THE
BIBLE
RECAP
STUDY GUIDE

Books by Tara-Leigh Cobble

*The Bible Recap: A One-Year Guide to Reading
and Understanding the Entire Bible*

*The Bible Recap Study Guide: Daily Questions to Deepen Your
Understanding of the Entire Bible*

The Bible Recap Journal: Your Daily Companion to the Entire Bible

*The Bible Recap Discussion Guide: Weekly Questions for Group
Conversation on the Entire Bible*

*The Bible Recap Kids' Devotional: 365 Reflections and Activities
for Children and Families*

The God Shot: 100 Snapshots of God's Character in Scripture

Israel: Beauty, Light, and Luxury

THE
BIBLE
RECAP
STUDY GUIDE

Daily Questions to Deepen
Your Understanding of
THE ENTIRE BIBLE

TARA-LEIGH COBBLE

BETHANY HOUSE
a division of Baker Publishing Group
Minneapolis, Minnesota

© 2021 by Tara-Leigh Cobble

Published by Bethany House Publishers
Minneapolis, Minnesota
www.bethanyhouse.com

Bethany House Publishers is a division of
Baker Publishing Group, Grand Rapids, Michigan

Printed in the United States of America

Library of Congress Cataloging-in-Publication Data
Names: Cobble, Tara Leigh, author.
Title: The Bible recap study guide : daily questions to deepen your understanding of the entire
    Bible / Tara-Leigh Cobble.
Description: Minneapolis, Minnesota : Bethany House, a division of Baker Publishing Group,
    [2021]
Identifiers: LCCN 2021033775 | ISBN 9780764240324 (paperback)
Subjects: LCSH: Bible—Examinations, questions, etc.
Classification: LCC BS612 .C56 2021 | DDC 220—dc23
LC record available at https://lccn.loc.gov/2021033775

Cover design by Rob Williams, InsideOut Creative Arts, Inc.

The Bible Recap logo design by Landon Wade

The author is represented by Alive Literary Agency, www.aliveliterary.com.

Baker Publishing Group publications use paper produced from sustainable forestry practices and post-consumer waste whenever possible.

24 25 26 27 28 29   10 9 8 7 6

Contents

How to Use This Guide and Other Tools

First, please visit **thebiblerecap.com/start**. It will tell you all you need to know to join our reading plan and podcast. Then, we recommend doing the following steps each day, in this order:

1. Do your daily Bible reading according to The Bible Recap reading plan you've chosen: whole Bible (Old Testament and New Testament) or New Testament only.
2. Use the *The Bible Recap Journal* during your reading.
3. Use this daily study guide after (or during) your reading. We've left room underneath the questions where you can write your answers in the guide itself.
4. Listen to the corresponding podcast episode or read the entry in *The Bible Recap* book for more information, insights, and answers.
5. Use the *Weekly Discussion Guide*, available at thebiblerecap.com, in group conversations about that week's reading plan. Since these questions are intended for group discussion, we did not aim to create space for answering in the weekly guide itself.

The journal is intended to be self-guided, while the daily and weekly guides offer a higher level of challenge and connection. You don't have to have both guides (this daily study guide and the *Weekly Discussion Guide*), but we created them with the intention of complementing each other. This daily study guide's questions tend to focus more on research and study, whereas the weekly discussion guide's questions are more reflective and suited for personal discussion. If anyone in your discussion group is also using the journal or this guide, it can help further your conversation to ask for their input from what they've learned there as well.

In order to connect with and challenge all types of readers, we've offered a variety of questions throughout these guides—objective, subjective, and critical thinking, as well as questions to help you sharpen your research skills. For those questions in the latter category, we've listed some tools below that you may find helpful.

Helpful Resources

Here are some free resources we've used in researching and writing this study and the podcast. You may also find it helpful to purchase a physical copy of a study Bible or commentary. Some of our current favorites for broad use are the ESV Study Bible, *Matthew Henry's Commentary on the Whole Bible*, the Arthur W. Pink commentaries, and the Douglas J. Moo commentaries.

Study Bible: bible.faithlife.com

Commentaries: biblestudytools.com

Hebrew and Greek lexicon: blueletterbible.org

Other websites: bibleproject.com, gotquestions.org, biblecharts.org, desiringgod.org

While we can't offer a blanket endorsement of everything produced by these sites and resources (especially as content may change over time), we generally find them to be trustworthy and helpful.

DAY 1 / GENESIS 1–3

1. Who wrote Genesis?

2. To or for whom was it written?

3. When was it written?

4. What is the literary style (narrative, history, wisdom, prophecy, letter, etc.)?

5. Who does "us" refer to in 1:26? (Consider Genesis 1:2, John 1:1–3, and Colossians 1:16–20.)

6. How are humans different from everything else God created?

7. What is the difference between something being "good" or "very good" (1:31) and something being "perfect"? How does man's imperfection correspond to the fall of mankind and our need for Jesus (Hebrews 10:14)?

8. What false belief is at the root of Eve's response to temptation?

9. How do the first humans respond to God when they sin? What does God do when they sin?

DAY 2 / GENESIS 4–7

1. How could Cain know that murdering Abel is wrong (4:14) if God hasn't given the Ten Commandments yet?

2. What does it mean for God to be sorry and "grieved" (6:6)? Use a Hebrew lexicon to look up those words in the original language. Does this imply that God made a bad choice or did something wrong? Why or why not?

3. What do you think the term "sons of God" means in 6:4? Look up possible interpretations in a commentary or study Bible and write what you find.

4. Look up the term "covenant" (6:18) in a dictionary or Bible dictionary and write down the definition.

DAY 3 / GENESIS 8–11

1. Review 8:16–17, 9:1, and 9:7. Write out the specific instructions from each verse. To whom or to what does each set of instructions apply?

2. With whom does God make this covenant (9:8–10)?

3. What does God promise about the earth in this covenant (8:21–22, 9:11–17)?

4. How does man's relationship with animals change after the flood (9:2–4)?

5. In 11:4, what are the people of Babel trying to accomplish? And what are they trying to avoid?

DAY 4 / JOB 1–5

1. Who wrote Job?

2. To or for whom was it written?

3. When was it written?

4. What is the literary style (narrative, history, wisdom, prophecy, letter, etc.)?

5. Is there a connection between the "sons of God" in Job 1:6 and those in Genesis 6:4?

6. Look up the word "Satan" (1:8) in a Hebrew lexicon. What does it mean, and how is it used elsewhere in Scripture?

7. How would you describe Job's perspective after all he's lost?

8. Who does Eliphaz imply gave him the "words of wisdom" he's speaking (4:12–21)?

9. Eliphaz offers his opinion, which means it could be right, wrong, or a combination of the two. Identify one part you know or believe to be true about God (based on what the rest of Scripture says).

DAY 5 / JOB 6–9

1. Job expresses his confusion; he wrestles with the cause of his pain and how to put an end to it. Is there a way we can tell the difference between punishment, discipline, an attack of the enemy, and just life's hard circumstances?

2. What does Bildad think is the root of Job's troubles?

3. Look up the word "mercy" (9:15) and write down the definition.

DAY 6 / JOB 10–13

1. What does Zophar think Job needs to do in order to solve his troubles? Is he right? Why or why not?

2. Who does Job ultimately hold responsible for his troubles (12:9)? Why?

3. Where does Job look for hope? Why?

4. How would you summarize Job's feelings and posture toward God?

DAY 7 / JOB 14–16

1. How would you summarize Eliphaz's tone toward Job in chapter 15?

2. Job references "Sheol" regularly. Look up that word in a Hebrew lexicon to get some potential definitions for what he's referring to. Strong's lexicon (on blueletterbible.org) is particularly helpful.

3. Have Job's friends succeeded in easing his pain with their words of counsel? Why or why not?

DAY 8 / JOB 17–20

1. Describe Job's attitude toward his friends in chapter 17. Describe Bildad's attitude toward Job in chapter 18.

2. Find a verse in chapter 19 where Job might inadvertently prophesy about Jesus. How is this prophecy fulfilled?

3. In 20:3, Zophar claims a spirit guided his words to Job. If you were Job, how would Zophar's words land on you?

4. Do Zophar's accusations toward Job in 20:12–29 line up with what we know about Job from chapter 1? Why or why not?

DAY 9 / JOB 21–23

1. In chapter 21, Job not only wrestles with why bad things have happened to him, but he also wrestles with why good things happen to the wicked. Which idea troubles you more? Why?

2. Given that things seem "unfair" in life, how does that speak to the notion of karma? What truths from Scripture seem to correspond to or contradict the idea of karma?

3. In 22:13–14, Eliphaz falsely accuses Job of calling God ignorant and impotent. Look back at Job's words in chapter 19 and find at least one place where he said the opposite of what Eliphaz claims.

4. Are Job's words in 23:14 more terrifying or more comforting to you? Why?

DAY 10 / JOB 24–28

1. In chapter 24, Job spends a lot of time addressing the concerns and struggles of the poor, even though he has been very rich. What does this reveal about his character? In what ways does this mirror Jesus?

2. In 25:4, Bildad claims that it's impossible for a man to be righteous. Is this true? Why or why not?

3. Find a verse in chapter 26 where Job inadvertently prophesies about Jesus. Where is this prophecy fulfilled?

4. Look up the name "Rahab" (26:12) in a Hebrew lexicon. What possible definitions are given? Which seems most likely?

5. Job's friends continue to implore him to repent, heightening their argument. According to what we know of the story and what he says in 27:3–6, why does he refuse?

6. In chapter 28, Job searches for wisdom. Where does he find it? How would you describe it?

1. Considering all Job has lost, how frequently does he refer to his former possessions or wealth? What are the things he seems to mourn losing the most?

2. In chapter 31, Job considers all his ways to see if there's any unknown sin in his heart or life. He offers just responses to any potential sin. Circle every "if" in your Bible, then read each "if" statement, taking time to consider whether any resonate with you personally. If so, spend some time in repentance and ask for God's help to desire better things.

3. For each "if" statement, consider what it reveals about what God loves and hates. Write a list of each. (Hint: The things God hates oppose or violate what He loves. For instance, God hates pride because He loves humility, etc.)

DAY 12 / JOB 32–34

1. Describe Elihu based on what we see about him in 32:1–5. At this point in the reading, do you think you'll agree with what he says? Why or why not?

2. Do you see any verse(s) in this speech that points to Elihu's possible humility? What about possible arrogance?

3. In 33:19–30, Elihu claims that God uses trials as a means to produce repentance. How have you seen this in your own life? What aspects of God's character are revealed in this?

4. Is Elihu's opinion of Job's problem different from that of Job's three other friends? If so, how?

DAY 13 / JOB 35–37

1. Summarize the two complementary statements Elihu makes in 35:5–7.

2. In 36:1–4 Elihu claims to be speaking on God's behalf. Based on what we've read so far, does he seem to be right or wrong in this claim? Why or why not?

3. "The godless in heart cherish anger" (36:13). Think of a time when you cherished anger. What were you angry about? Was it something that angers God too? Did cherishing anger draw you closer to God?

4. In 36:21, Elihu seems to be saying that people use pain as an excuse to sin. Give some examples (personal or generalized) of how this might manifest.

DAY 14 / JOB 38–39

1. Finally, God speaks! But He doesn't answer any of the questions Job has been asking. What does He do instead?

2. What can we learn about God and our circumstances based on the way He responds to Job?

3. Did you see a prophecy about Jesus in the LORD's words today? What does this statement reveal about the divinity of Jesus?

DAY 15 / JOB 40–42

1. Summarize what Job says when he finally responds to God in chapter 40.

2. Look up "Behemoth" (40:15) and "Leviathan" (41:1) in a Hebrew lexicon and record what you find.

3. How would you summarize God's theme in chapters 40–41?

4. God is a peacemaker—He enters into chaos and creates peace. Describe His process of peacemaking as demonstrated in 42:7–9. List the relationships where peace is made.

5. Does anything stand out as unique or noteworthy about the genealogy in 42:13–15?

DAY 16 / GENESIS 12–15

1. Why does God bless Abram? What lesson can we take from this?

2. Who is Abram trying to protect by misleading Pharaoh?

3. Visual search: Look at a map of ancient Israel and locate the Dead Sea. Sodom would've been near Zoar, at the southern end of the Dead Sea. This is where Lot lived (13:12). Now locate the city of Dan, near the north of Israel. This is where Abram chased Lot's pursuers to get him back (14:14).

4. Write down four facts about Melchizedek and his actions.

5. At this point in the story, what two tangible things does God promise to give Abram as a part of His blessing on him? Cite references.

DAY 17 / GENESIS 16–18

1. Look up the word "angel" in a Hebrew lexicon and write down what you find.

2. In chapter 16, what actions, statements, or descriptors point to the Angel of the LORD being God Himself?

3. Circumcision affects the most personal part of a man's anatomy, which also happens to be the means by which he bears offspring. How is this a fitting symbol for God's relationship with the Israelites?

4. In chapter 18, God seems to appear to Abraham as a man. Angels have also appeared as men. What actions, statements, or descriptors point to this being God, not just any man or angel?

DAY 18 / GENESIS 19–21

1. In 19:5, the men of Sodom demand to have sex with the visiting angels (who appear as men). Can you think of another passage from Genesis that is similar to this situation? What happened in that instance?

2. Look up Ezekiel 16:49–50. What does it list as Sodom's chief sin? How do you see that demonstrated in today's text from Genesis?

3. How many righteous people are in Sodom after all? Is Lot righteous? Read 2 Peter 2:7 and write out any questions or new insights you gain.

4. Why do you think Abraham lies to King Abimelech in the same way he lied to Pharaoh? What lesson has he failed to learn?

5. Look up the word "prophet" (Genesis 20:7) in a dictionary or Bible dictionary and write down what you find.

DAY 19 / GENESIS 22-24

1. Since each Bible version translates things differently, look up Genesis 22:2 in a Hebrew lexicon. Then write down the English translation of God's command to Abraham. Does this vary from the way the command is translated in the version you're reading? If so, how?

2. Based on Genesis 22:2, where does God tell Abraham to offer this sacrifice? Be as specific as the text allows.

3. Review 22:13. What images foreshadow Jesus in this story of God's provision of a sacrifice? Explain.

4. Review 23:19–20. Where does Abraham bury Sarah? Why is this significant?

DAY 20 / GENESIS 25–26

1. Verse 25:18 says Abraham's son Ishmael settles "over against all his kinsmen." Look this verse up in a Hebrew lexicon or a Bible dictionary and write down what it indicates.

2. How does this correspond to what was prophesied about him in Genesis 16:12?

3. In chapter 26, how does Isaac manifest the sins of his father Abraham? Of all the people involved in this sin, who seems to understand the gravity of it most?

4. How old is Isaac when he marries Rebekah?

5. What part of the prophecy in 25:23 goes against the cultural norms of the day?

DAY 21 / GENESIS 27–29

1. Describe Rebekah's demeanor based on what we see in chapter 27.

2. How does Isaac refer to YHWH in 27:20? How does YHWH refer to Himself in 28:13? Why might this be significant?

3. How would you summarize Jacob's statement after he builds the pillar in 28:20–22?

4. How does Laban give Jacob a taste of his own medicine?

5. Write down the meanings of the names of Leah's four sons in order. Based on these names, what seems to be happening in her heart through this process?

DAY 22 / GENESIS 30–31

1. Write down the meanings of Leah's sons' names, including those by Zilpah. Write down the meanings of Rachel's sons' names, including those by Bilhah. Do any themes emerge?

2. How would you describe the actions and attitudes of Rachel and Leah? What seems to be at the heart of their struggle? How does God respond?

3. Why does Rachel want the mandrakes? Look up "mandrakes" in a Hebrew lexicon or use a search engine for historical context.

4. Read Exodus 21:1–2. This is the agreement Jacob has been living under for two back-to-back terms as an indentured servant or slave to Laban. Based on this agreement, Jacob is free to go after fourteen years, plus God has called him to go back to Canaan. But both Jacob and Laban rebel against God and His ways for the

next six years. What motivates their disobedience? Whose plans end up succeeding? How?

5. In both 31:42 and 31:53, Jacob refers to God as "the Fear of Isaac." *Gesenius' Hebrew-Chaldee Lexicon* says this means "reverence" here. In what way did Jacob's father, Isaac, show reverence to YHWH?

DAY 23 / GENESIS 32–34

1. How would you describe the tone of Jacob's prayer in 32:9–12?

2. Look up the word "prevailed" (32:28) in a Hebrew lexicon and write down the possible definitions. Which definition seems to apply here, given the context?

3. What is significant about God changing Jacob's name here?

4. What does Jacob build in 33:20? How is this different from what he has built in the past? What is significant about the name he gives it?

5. Is the story in chapter 34 descriptive or prescriptive? Does it describe what happens or does it tell us these actions were the right actions?

DAY 24 / GENESIS 35–37

1. Look up the word "terror" (35:5) in a Hebrew lexicon. Where else in Scripture is this word used?

2. Read Genesis 28:18–22. Compare it to what happens here in 35:6–7. What does this reveal about Jacob's heart?

3. According to 36:8, what's the other name for Esau and his descendants?

4. Which of Jacob's wives or concubines gave birth to his favorite son, Joseph?

5. Look up 37:3 in a Hebrew lexicon. Describe Joseph's garment based on the meanings of the original language.

DAY 25 / GENESIS 38–40

1. Considering ancient Near Eastern culture, why does Tamar need to be married? What would happen if she remained unmarried with no children?

2. Why might Judah hesitate to let her marry his third son?

3. Describe Judah's attitude before and after having his sins publicly exposed.

4. Look for a theme in chapter 39. What comforting fact is repeated four times throughout Joseph's various struggles?

5. Read Matthew 1:1–6. What does this reveal about God in light of what we read today?

DAY 26 / GENESIS 41–42

1. The most common scenario with biblical dream-signs is for the dreamer to also serve as the interpreter. However, neither of Joseph's cellmates nor Pharaoh are able to give their own interpretations. What might account for this?

2. Where did Joseph get his gift for dream interpretation?

3. Write down the meanings of the names of Joseph's sons. What does this suggest about his heart and attitude?

4. Decades after Joseph's brothers sold him into slavery, they are still dwelling in the guilt of what they've done to him (42:21) and fearing punishment from God, even though they seem to feel repentant about their sin. How can we rightly view our sins and guilt but not dwell in shame or condemnation?

DAY 27 / GENESIS 43–45

1. What about what happens in 43:33 causes the brothers to be "in amazement"?

2. Why might it be that Joseph gives Benjamin a greater portion?

3. Review 44:18–34. How would you describe Judah's speech? What role did he play in what happened to Joseph? What else do we know about Judah and his story?

4. Verses 45:1–9 reveal the heart of a person who forgives easily. What traits describe that kind of heart? What characteristics define that kind of person?

DAY 28 / GENESIS 46–47

1. Review 46:3. What promise does God make to Jacob about Egypt?

2. Why might Jacob want to stop in Beersheba on their way to Egypt? What significance does this place hold for him? (Use a concordance to look up previous occurrences of Beersheba in Scripture.)

3. Why does Joseph want his family to live in Goshen? Why does Pharaoh want them to live there?

4. How does Jacob describe the days of his life in 47:9? What things that we've seen from his life point to these descriptors?

5. Why is Jacob so emphatic about what happens to his body after his death?

DAY 29 / GENESIS 48–50

1. Do a web search for a list of the twelve tribes of Israel (Jacob) and write down each of the names.

2. What do you notice about this list that pertains to Jacob's two main speeches today (chapters 48 and 49)?

3. How does the story of Jacob's grandsons parallel his own story with his brother Esau (48:8–20)?

4. Why does Jacob retract the primary blessing (reserved for the first-born) from his three oldest sons? Which son does the blessing land on? Read Micah 5:2 and Matthew 1:1–16. What's noteworthy about these connections?

5. What request does Joseph make for his burial?

DAY 30 / EXODUS 1–3

1. Who wrote Exodus?

2. To or for whom was it written?

3. When was it written?

4. What is the literary style (narrative, history, wisdom, prophecy, letter, etc.)?

5. Why are the Hebrew midwives honored for (likely) lying? What does this reveal about God?

6. How does Pharaoh's oppression impact the numbers of the Hebrew population?

7. According to Exodus 2:1–10, which of the twelve tribes of Israel (Jacob) is Moses from?

8. How would you summarize each of Moses' excuses today when God appoints him?

DAY 31 / EXODUS 4–6

1. How would you summarize each of Moses' excuses today when God appoints him?

2. God promises opposition from Pharaoh but says Moses will eventually succeed at rescuing the Israelites out of slavery. According to 3:20–22, what will they take with them when they go?

3. Based on what relieves God's anger in 4:25–26, why is God angry in 4:24? Why was this so important? Use a study Bible or commentary for help if you need it.

4. When Moses and Aaron get to Egypt and obey God's commands, do things get better or worse?

5. Review 6:6–8 and list all the things God says He will do for the Israelites as a group. What does He ask of them in return?

6. According to 6:9, why don't the people believe Moses when he tells them about God's promises?

DAY 32 / EXODUS 7–9

1. What happens when Pharaoh calls in his magicians during plagues one and two? Are they able to stop or reverse the plagues?

2. Why did God raise Pharaoh to a position of power? What is the ultimate purpose of Pharaoh's leadership?

3. How does God treat the servants of Pharaoh in 9:20–21? What does this reveal about God?

4. How many plagues does it take for Pharaoh to finally admit his sin? Is his admission indicative of genuine repentance?

5. In 9:29–30, how does Moses respond to Pharaoh's admission of guilt?

DAY 33 / EXODUS 10–12

1. In 10:7, even Pharaoh's servants plead with him to let the people go. He appears to listen to them at first. Why do you think he ultimately refuses?

2. Some of the plagues are location-specific or only affect the Egyptians. What do you think God is emphasizing by drawing this distinction (11:7)?

3. Look at a doorframe. Imagine dipping a branch of leaves into blood to paint a mark on the left side and the right side, and also on the lintel, or top beam (12:7, 22–23). What image would this create as the blood drips down from the top beam? What does this foreshadow?

4. Review 3:20–22. What specific promises that seemed impossible does God fulfill in chapter 12?

5. According to 12:40, how long did the Israelites live in Egypt? Review the promise God made Abram in Genesis 15:13. Did God break His promise? What might account for this distinction?

Week 5 / Day 33 / Exodus 10–12

DAY 34 / EXODUS 13–15

1. In 13:9 and 13:16, where does Moses tell the Israelites to commemorate God's rescue?

2. According to 13:17–18, why does God send the Israelites the long way around?

3. Although Moses is the leader of the Israelites, who is actually guiding and directing their steps? Cite some of the verses where you see this referenced in today's reading.

4. Practically speaking, how would a cloud be helpful in the desert during the day? How would a pillar of fire be helpful in the desert at night?

5. In 14:1–3, when God warns Moses that Pharaoh is coming, what directions does He give him for preparation? And what does 14:4 say about God's motive for giving these instructions?

DAY 35 / EXODUS 16–18

1. How would you summarize the Israelites' attitude in 16:1–8? How does God respond to their actions in 16:9? And in 16:12?

2. What practical purpose does the manna serve? What spiritual purpose does the manna serve? What other symbolic or eternal purposes might also be served through the manna?

3. What instructions does God give Moses for getting water in 17:6?

4. What theme do you see in the stories from 17:12 and 18:18–23?

5. Review 18:1 and 18:10–12. Who are the Midianites? Why is Jethro's story significant?

DAY 36 / EXODUS 19–21

1. List all the natural phenomena and events that happen as God descends on the mountain in 19:16–20. Describe the scene. What does God ask Moses to do in the midst of all this?

2. As God delivers the Ten Commandments to Moses in chapter 20, how does He begin the conversation? What might God be emphasizing by opening this way?

3. How would you summarize the theme of the first four commandments? How would you summarize the theme of the final six commandments?

4. In the second commandment (20:4–6), does the emphasis seem to be on not making the object or not worshipping the object? Or both?

5. Look up the word "jealous" (20:5) in a Hebrew lexicon and write down what you find. (*Gesenius' Hebrew-Chaldee Lexicon* on blueletterbible.org is especially helpful here.)

DAY 37 / EXODUS 22–24

1. Review 22:1, 22:4, and 22:7. For each verse, write down how much was stolen and how much God ordered as repayment. Why might God set things up this way?

2. According to Deuteronomy 22:25, the penalty for rape is death. How is what's described in Exodus 22:16–17 different?

3. Look up the word "sojourner" in a dictionary, Bible dictionary, and/or Hebrew lexicon. Write down what you find.

4. Review 22:21–27 and 23:4–9. What do these verses reveal about God's heart?

5. Review 24:7–8. What kind of message or symbolism does it seem like Moses is communicating through his actions in 24:8?

1. Use a study Bible or search engine to find the length of a cubit. Based on the measurements listed in 25:10, determine the height, width, and depth of the ark of the covenant. To help visualize its size, think of a common object that has roughly the same dimensions and write it down.

2. One gold cherub is carved on each end of the mercy seat (25:18–19). Cherubim are unique heavenly creatures that are described in great detail in Ezekiel 1 and 10. Read Ezekiel 1:5–18 and write down a brief summary of the description he gives.

3. Look up the word "meet" (25:22) in a Hebrew lexicon. What are some other common uses for this word? Based on the other meanings, what picture does that give us of the beauty of this mercy seat?

4. Throughout today's reading, God orders the people to make things "of one piece" or "a single whole." Why might this be important symbolically or practically?

DAY 39 / EXODUS 28–29

1. According to 28:3, who equips the skilled with their skills? How?

2. Look up the word "holy" in a dictionary or Bible dictionary and write down the definition. If there are any words in the definition that you can't define, look those up too.

3. Look up "Urim" and "Thummim" (28:30) in a Hebrew lexicon and summarize what you find.

4. Look up the word "consecrate" in a dictionary or Bible dictionary and write down the definition. If there are any words in the definition that you can't define, look those up too.

5. Review 29:19–20. Can you think of any symbolic or practical reasons why the tip of the ear, finger, and toe are the chosen spots for marking the priests with blood?

DAY 40 / EXODUS 30–32

1. Do a web search to see how much a biblical half shekel is worth in today's money. This one-time census tax serves as a ransom for their lives (30:12, 16). What does this fixed-rate tax reveal about God's heart for His people?

2. Bezalel is called to craft things for God's dwelling place. Review Exodus 20:4–6. Why isn't Bezalel's work sinful?

3. How do the people view God's timing in meeting with Moses (32:1)? How does God view the timing (32:7–8)? What can we learn from this?

4. Review 32:1–6. Going verse by verse, trace the root of their sin to its full-blown manifestation in idolatry. What lies are they believing about God that lead to their eventual idolatry?

5. In 32:7–35, God sees the people worshipping a golden calf and wants to destroy them all. Moses begs Him to relent. Moments later, Moses sees it with his own eyes, rages with fury, and punishes them all. Later, God punishes the guilty specifically. What does this juxtaposition of God's response and Moses' response reveal to us about God?

DAY 41 / **EXODUS 33–35**

1. What's the name of the structure and location where Moses meets with God to talk (33:7)? Summarize how this structure and location are different from the tabernacle God recently instructed them to build for Him (25:8–9 specifically, plus all of chapters 25–30 in general).

2. Look up the word "face" (33:11) in a Hebrew lexicon. What other definitions are offered here that help build out our understanding of what this means?

3. In 33:16, what does Moses list as the thing that makes this people unique?

4. Exodus 34:6–7 is the passage quoted most frequently elsewhere in Scripture. It is God's description of Himself. Write down each adjective or description in the order they appear in the text. Do any of these traits seem undesirable or unrighteous to you? If so, is there any explanation for how that could still fit with God's character? Use a study Bible if you need help.

5. The Israelites are former slaves living in the desert. Where did they get the things described in 35:4–19 that are used to build the tabernacle?

DAY 42 / EXODUS 36–38

1. Read Hebrews 9:23–24 (and the surrounding context, if it's helpful). Twice in these verses, the author calls the tabernacle a "copy" of something else. What is it a copy of?

2. According to 36:2–7, how much do the people bring to contribute to the tabernacle?

3. Write a list of the seven pieces of furniture in the tabernacle, with each piece listed on its own line.

4. Beside each piece of furniture, write its practical purpose.

5. Besides its practical purpose, write its spiritual significance. Use a study Bible if you need help.

DAY 43 / EXODUS 39–40

1. Look up the word "ephod" (39:2) in a dictionary or Bible dictionary and write what you learn about its physical description.

2. Look up the word "anoint" (40:9) in a dictionary or Bible dictionary and write what you find.

3. What purpose is served by anointing the furniture, the utensils and tools, and the priests with oil?

4. What does oil represent in Scripture? Use a study Bible, Bible dictionary, or web search for help if you need to.

DAY 44 / LEVITICUS 1–4

1. Who wrote Leviticus?

2. To or for whom was it written?

3. When was it written?

4. What is the literary style (narrative, history, wisdom, prophecy, letter, etc.)?

5. The word "atonement" shows up a lot in today's reading (1:4, 4:20, 4:26, 4:31, 4:35). Look up the word in a dictionary or Bible dictionary and write what you find. If there are any words in the definition that you can't define, look those up too.

6. Primarily, sacrifice serves as a "covering" for sin in the spiritual realm. In 2:3 and 2:10 we see a secondary purpose for offerings and sacrifices. What practical purpose do they serve?

7. Is unintentional sin something God overlooks? Why or why not?

DAY 45 / LEVITICUS 5–7

1. In your own words, explain each of these states: unclean, clean, holy, perfect.

2. Can you be unclean without sinning? Does being unclean carry legal guilt with it? Explain and cite Scripture.

3. How is God's heart for His people revealed in the compensation required for certain sins (5:5–13)?

4. Review 7:19–27. What does the phrase "that person shall be cut off from his people" mean? Does it apply to sin or uncleanness? Use a study Bible if you prefer.

5. Based on what you learned from question 4, what does this reveal about God's motives?

DAY 46 / LEVITICUS 8–10

1. Look up the word "ordain" (8:33) in a dictionary or Bible dictionary and write down the definition. If there are any words in the definition that you can't define, look those up too.

2. Moses anoints, consecrates, and ordains Aaron and his sons in today's reading. Briefly summarize the purpose of each of these three steps.

3. Whose sins does the priest have to atone for first—his own or the people's (9:7–18)? Why is this order important?

4. Look up the word "unauthorized" (10:1) in a Hebrew lexicon and write down what you find. What do this verse and definition suggest about where Nadab and Abihu went wrong?

5. How does Aaron display humility and teachability in chapter 10? How does Moses display humility and teachability in chapter 10?

DAY 47 / LEVITICUS 11–13

1. Why might God forbid people from eating animals that died on their own? Doesn't it seem more cruel to kill an animal to eat it than to eat one that is already dead?

2. How is God's heart for His people revealed in the required offerings for purification after childbirth (12:6–8)?

3. Read Luke 2:22–24. What does this reveal to us about the parents of Jesus?

4. God's instructions to this new society are detailed and lengthy. Is God just trying to micromanage them? What motive might be behind all these instructions?

5. Look up the word "leprous" (13:2) in a Hebrew lexicon. What other items can this word apply to besides the human body?

DAY 48 / LEVITICUS 14–15

1. If uncleanness isn't always related to sin, why are offerings required of those who have been made clean?

2. If uncleanness isn't always related to sin, what is the purpose of distancing the unclean person from the rest of society? Is it punishment? Protection? Something else?

3. In 14:34, who does God ultimately hold responsible for leprosy of the house?

4. At this point, the Israelites are living in the desert in tents, but God is giving instructions for how to deal with problems that will exist in their future houses in the promised land. Why is God addressing a problem they don't even have yet? What might be His motive?

DAY 49 / LEVITICUS 16–18

1. According to 16:29–31, what does God command the people to do while the priest is atoning for their sins?

2. Using a study Bible or a web search, look up the phrase "afflict yourselves" (16:29) and write down what you find. Then, look up the words in a Hebrew lexicon for comparison.

3. Did you see any foreshadowing of Jesus in today's reading? Explain. Where is this foreshadowing fulfilled?

4. What does God call the false gods they've been sacrificing to in 17:7?

5. Besides morality, what other purpose(s) do the laws on sexual activity serve?

DAY 50 / LEVITICUS 19–21

1. Review 19:9–10. Then read Ruth 2:2–16. How does Boaz demonstrate God's heart toward the poor? Does he do precisely what this law from today's reading requires of him?

2. What is particularly cruel or specifically oppressive about the three examples of sin listed in 19:13–14?

3. Review 19:17–18. What two parts of this law indicate that God is interested in more than just how we act?

4. While 21:21 feels like harsh treatment of those who are blemished, God hasn't banished them from His presence or His people. In fact, He offers an invitation and a piece of consolation in 21:22–23. What are they?

5. Look up the word "sanctifies" (21:23) in a Bible dictionary and write the definition in your own words.

DAY 51 / LEVITICUS 22–23

1. What phrase does God repeat three times in 22:9–32? What might He be trying to emphasize?

2. What phrase does God repeat five times in chapter 22? What might He be trying to emphasize?

3. Write a list of the seven feasts (including the weekly feast of the Sabbath) in chapter 23. Take note of any details that help you understand the purpose of each feast.

4. Review 23:42–43. Why does God tell the Israelites to live in booths (tents) during this feast?

DAY 52 / LEVITICUS 24–25

1. What does 24:21 reveal or reiterate about how humans are distinct from other living things? How is this reflected in Genesis 1:26–28?

2. Review 25:17 and 25:43. Each verse lists a pair of opposite actions. How or why are they opposites?

3. How often does the Year of Jubilee happen?

4. Look up the word "jubilee" (25:10) in a Hebrew lexicon and write down what you find.

5. In the Sabbath year, God commands the people not to farm their land. How does He plan to provide for them if they aren't farming during that year (25:18–22)?

DAY 53 / LEVITICUS 26–27

1. In chapter 26, God lays out some of the terms of His covenant with the Israelites. Covenantal agreements often end with blessings for keeping the covenant and consequences of breaking the covenant. Summarize three blessings of keeping the covenant.

2. Summarize three consequences of breaking the covenant.

3. God uses the word "discipline" three times in chapter 26. Find and circle them in your Bible or write down the references. Write down anything you notice about the repeated use and context.

4. God uses the word "remember" four times in chapter 26. Find and circle them in your Bible or write down the references. Write down anything you notice about the repeated use and context.

5. Based on the trajectory of chapter 26, what seems to be the point of the discipline God will send when the Israelites break the covenant with Him?

DAY 54 / NUMBERS 1–2

1. Who wrote Numbers?

2. To or for whom was it written?

3. When was it written?

4. What is the literary style (narrative, history, wisdom, prophecy, letter, etc.)?

5. God orders Moses to take a census. Taking a census is often a step toward preparing for war, so you can know how large your army will be. Given what you know so far, who do you think God might be preparing the Israelites to fight against?

6. Which of the tribes is the largest?

DAY 55 / NUMBERS 3–4

1. Which two people are appointed as heads of the tabernacle?

2. Which tribe does God claim as "His own" and His "firstborn"?

3. What were the names of Levi's three sons (3:17)?

4. How would you summarize the unique roles of each of the three clans of the Levites (Kohathites, Merarites, Gershonites)?

5. Each Levite was appointed to one of two types of service listed in 4:46–49. What are they?

DAY 56 / NUMBERS 5–6

1. Read Deuteronomy 22:22. What is the penalty for adultery under the law? How are the laws we read in 5:11–31 different from that law?

2. Why might the female be the subject of this test instead of the male?

3. In this test or judgment, who is ultimately called to act as a witness?

4. Is the Nazirite vow generally a temporary or permanent vow?

5. What things does God command a person to avoid when he or she takes the Nazirite vow?

DAY 57 / NUMBERS 7

1. What do the chiefs of the tribes of Israel give to the tabernacle?

2. What are these offerings used for (7:5)?

3. Which two clans of the Levites get to use them?

4. Why aren't any given to the Kohathites?

5. The tribes vary widely in number but still bring gifts of the same value to the Levites for the tabernacle. What do you think this is intended to convey or symbolize?

DAY 58 / **NUMBERS 8–10**

1. What is conveyed or symbolized by the people putting their hands on the Levites? In what other scenario is this same thing done (8:5–13)?

2. When does God consecrate ("set apart as holy") the Levites for Himself (8:14–18)? What have the Levites done to earn this position of honor from God?

3. What two roles do the Levites serve (8:19)?

4. What instructions does God give to the men who are unclean for Passover (9:6–12)?

5. What is God demonstrating by opening up the Passover celebration to non-Israelites (9:14)?

DAY 59 / NUMBERS 11–13

1. What are the Israelites grumbling about in 11:1–10? What does God say is the root of all their grumbling (11:20)?

2. What does God do to help Moses deal with the people and their complaints (11:17)? How does Moses feel about this (11:29)?

3. Use a study Bible or a search engine to find out how much a homer holds in today's measurements (11:32). Based on that information, how much does each person gather at minimum?

4. Use a Hebrew lexicon to look up the name of the place where this grumbling and provision happen (11:34). What does the name mean?

5. Why don't Miriam and Aaron like Moses' wife? What does Moses do after Miriam's verbal attacks on his wife and God's response to her?

6. Ten of the twelve spies bring back a fearful report. What are their fears based on? What are they specifically focused on, considering their words in 13:31 and 13:33? Is there anything crucial they're forgetting in their report?

DAY 60 / NUMBERS 14–15; PSALM 90

1. Who wrote Psalms?

2. To or for whom was it written?

3. When was it written?

4. What is the literary style (narrative, history, wisdom, prophecy, letter, etc.)?

5. What consequences fall on the nation of Israel as a result of listening to the ten fear-filled spies?

6. What does God promise as a consequence for their sins in 14:35? What do the people wish for in 14:2?

7. Based on the context, how would you define doing something "with a high hand" (15:30)? Use a study Bible or a Hebrew lexicon for help if you need it.

DAY 61 / NUMBERS 16–17

1. What motive seems to be underneath Korah's rebellion?

2. How do Dathan and Abiram refer to Egypt (16:13)? How has God referred to Egypt (Exodus 20:2)? How has God referred to the promised land (Exodus 3:8)? What does this reveal about their hearts?

3. What promise is beginning to be fulfilled in the deaths of the 250 rebels and the plague that follows? Review 14:29–35 if you need help.

4. As high priest, why is it risky for Aaron to burn incense between the living and the dead?

5. What is made from the incense holders of the 250 rebels?

DAY 62 / NUMBERS 18–20

1. What parts of the tabernacle are Aaron's sons appointed to guard (18:5, 7)? What part of the tabernacle are the other Levites appointed to guard (18:3)?

2. Look up the word "tithe" (18:21) in a Hebrew lexicon and write down what you find.

3. Why do you think God is reiterating the laws about death and cleanliness in chapter 19?

4. What instructions does God give to Moses about getting water? How does Moses respond?

DAY 63 / NUMBERS 21–22

1. What is the turning point in the story of the snakes killing people (21:7)?

2. Does the serpent on the pole violate the second commandment? Why or why not?

3. According to John 3:14–15, what does this story foreshadow?

4. Look up 2 Kings 18:4. What eventually happens with the bronze serpent? Why?

5. A theme shows up three times in 22:3–5 that reveals why Balak doesn't like the Israelites. Write down what you see about the theme in each of those three verses.

6. What do you think is underneath God's seemingly conflicting counsel to Balaam?

7. What clues do we see in the text that the Angel of the LORD is God Himself (22:22–41)?

DAY 64 / NUMBERS 23–25

1. What pattern do you see in the way Balaam responds to Balak when he needs to hear clearly from God (22:8, 23:3, 23:15)?

2. The Israelites have no king at this point, but Balaam keeps referencing one as he speaks with King Balak (23:21, 24:7, 24:17). What or whom do you think Balaam is referring to in these oracles? Why?

3. How would you describe Balak's attitude during these exchanges between him and Balaam?

4. Read Genesis 12:3. What does this ultimately mean for Balak and for Balaam?

5. The last time there was a plague outbreak, Aaron the high priest intervened. Who intervened this time? What is their relationship?

DAY 65 / NUMBERS 26–27

1. Why is there a need for another census in chapter 26?

2. Why don't the Levites get an inheritance (26:62)? Review 18:20 for help if you need it.

3. The daughters of Zelophehad sought justice from Moses and God. What does this reveal about what they believed about God? What does God's response reveal about His heart?

4. Why doesn't Moses get to enter the promised land?

5. How does Moses respond when God tells him he won't enter the promised land?

DAY 66 / NUMBERS 28–30

1. What event bookends the Israelites' days? How does this vary on the Sabbath?

2. Is offering a sacrifice considered "work"? See 28:25, 29:12, and 29:35 if you need help.

3. Look up the word "vow" (30:2) in a Hebrew lexicon and write down what you find.

4. Why might God have the Israelites treat a married woman's vow differently from a married man's vow?

DAY 67 / NUMBERS 31–32

1. What is God's final assignment to Moses before his death?

2. Why did the Israelites kill Balaam?

3. Typically, after a battle is won, the women are kept alive. How and why is this situation with the Midianites different?

4. Visual search: Look at a map of ancient Israel. Locate the Mediterranean Sea and the Jordan River. Much of the land between these two areas is the promised land. Locate the land east of the Jordan River. In our timeline, this is where the Israelites are. Some of the tribes (Reuben, Gad, and half of Manasseh) want to stay here even though it isn't part of the promised land. This becomes known as the Transjordan ("across the Jordan").

5. What do these tribes promise Moses they'll do in order to be able to live in this land?

DAY 68 / NUMBERS 33–34

1. What idea does God repeat four times in His command in 33:52?

2. Why does God want them to be so thorough? What is His aim?

3. In 33:55, what is the consequence if they don't obey?

4. What landmark is referred to as the Salt Sea in 34:3? What landmark is referred to as the Great Sea in 34:7? Use a study Bible if you need help. Then locate these landmarks on a map of Israel.

5. Which tribes are excluded from the promise in 34:13? Why?

DAY 69 / NUMBERS 35–36

1. God didn't give the Levites a portion of land to live in. Where did He arrange for them to live?

2. In your own words, describe the purpose of a city of refuge.

3. In your own words, describe the distinction chapter 35 makes between being a "murderer" and a "manslayer."

4. What two types of people lived in the cities of refuge?

5. What guideline did Moses set up to make sure the daughters of Zelophehad retained their land?

DAY 70 / DEUTERONOMY 1–2

1. Who wrote Deuteronomy?

2. To or for whom was it written?

3. When was it written?

4. What is the literary style (narrative, history, wisdom, prophecy, letter, etc.)?

5. According to 1:2, how long would the Israelites' journey normally take? Why did it take them so much longer?

6. God doesn't promise to give the Israelites any and all land they want. He promises them a specific plot of land. To which two

other groups does He promise land? Why do you think these
groups are promised land as well (2:1–25)?

7. In a Hebrew lexicon, look up the words "Emim," "Anakim," and
"Rephaim" from 2:10–11 and write down what you find.

DAY 71 / DEUTERONOMY 3–4

1. When the Transjordan tribes (Reuben, Gad, the half tribe of Manasseh) go across the Jordan with the other tribes to drive out the Canaanites in the promised land, who or what is supposed to stay behind in the Transjordan?

2. Review 1:37 from yesterday and 3:26 and 4:21 today. Why does Moses say God shouldn't punish him? How would you describe Moses' perspective?

3. Write a list of the things Moses warns the people against worshipping.

4. In the covenant between God and the Israelites, what is the consequence of idolatry?

5. What does God say He will do if the people repent (4:29–31)?

DAY 72 / DEUTERONOMY 5–7

1. Why does God repeat the Ten Commandments in Deuteronomy 5 when He already gave them thirty-eight years earlier in Exodus 20?

2. Write out the prayer in 6:4–5.

3. Look up the word "one" (6:4) in a Hebrew lexicon. What other meanings of the word could apply here, given the context? Next, look up the word "heart" (6:5) and write down what you find.

4. Write a list of the verbs in 6:7–9. How would you summarize this list of God's commands?

5. What type of wrong thinking does Moses warn against in 7:17–18?

DAY 73 / DEUTERONOMY 8–10

1. Why did God keep the Israelites in the wilderness for forty years?

2. What type of wrong thinking does Moses warn against in 8:17–18?

3. What type of wrong thinking does Moses warn against in 9:4?

4. What are the reasons God is blessing the Israelites with the promised land (9:5)?

5. What do you think God means by the command in 10:16? Use a study Bible if you need help.

DAY 74 / DEUTERONOMY 11–13

1. Visual search: Locate Mount Gerizim and Mount Ebal on a map. They are located near Shechem, about halfway between the Jordan River (east) and the Mediterranean Sea (west), and halfway between the Sea of Galilee (north) and the Dead Sea (south).

2. Which mountain is the mountain of blessing, and which is the mountain of cursing (11:29)?

3. What general theme or command does Moses keep repeating?

4. Look up the word "Asherim" (12:3) in a Hebrew lexicon and write down what you find.

5. God's dwelling place will be in one specific place after they establish peace in the promised land (12:10–11). How is this different from what they've been experiencing in the wilderness?

6. What is the punishment for false prophets? Why is it important for their laws on this to be strict?

DAY 75 / DEUTERONOMY 14–16

1. Why is it important for the Israelites to avoid pagan practices when entering Canaan?

2. How does God ensure that the poor are cared for in Israel?

3. Given their history, why is it important for the nation of Israel not to be indebted to the nations around them?

4. If a Hebrew slave likes his master and decides to keep working for him even after working off his debt, how do they mark the agreement?

5. Three times in chapters 15–16, Moses tells the Israelites to remember something. What is it? Why do you think he wants them to remember it?

DAY 76 / DEUTERONOMY 17–20

1. Who carries out the death penalty in cases of worshipping false gods? Why do you think this is the standard?

2. What three things are Israel's future kings supposed to refrain from collecting? Why do you think this is the standard?

3. In what situations are soldiers excused from duty? What does this reveal about God, His power, and His heart?

4. Look up the phrase "purge the evil from your midst" (17:7, 17:12, 19:19) in a study Bible and write down what you find.

5. Compare Moses' use of this phrase to Paul's use of it in 1 Corinthians 5:13. How are the two uses similar? How are they different?

DAY 77 / DEUTERONOMY 21–23

1. Where do we see God's compassion for the foreign women in 21:10–14?

2. How does God give the woman the benefit of the doubt in the laws pertaining to rape, and particularly rape that occurs in the country?

3. What might God be trying to demonstrate by setting up laws where unique things were not intermingled with other things (seeds in a field, animals for plowing, fabrics in a garment, etc.)?

4. Did you see any foreshadowing of Jesus in today's reading? If so, where is it fulfilled?

DAY 78 / DEUTERONOMY 24–27

1. Given that God is always protective of His people and His name, what might be motivating the law about divorce in 24:1–4? Use a study Bible if you need help.

2. In 25:17, Moses commands the people to "remember Amalek." Review Exodus 17:8–16 and summarize what the Amalekites did to the Israelites.

3. Look up the phrase "first fruit" (26:10) in a Hebrew lexicon and write down what you find. What does bringing their firstfruits to God require of the Israelites?

4. Write two lists: the tribes on the Mount of Blessing and the tribes on the Mount of Cursing.

5. Did you see a prophecy related to Jesus in chapter 27? If so, where is it fulfilled?

DAY 79 / DEUTERONOMY 28–29

1. In 28:7, what does God claim to be sovereign over? In 28:11, what three things does God claim to be sovereign over?

2. God has commanded the Israelites to do lots of things, but what else does He promise to command in 28:8?

3. After God lists out the blessings for obeying the covenant, He lists out the curses for breaking it. What purpose do these curses serve?

4. According to 29:10–14, who is God making this covenant with?

DAY 80 / DEUTERONOMY 30–31

1. In 30:1, God seems to imply that the Israelites are going to break the covenant and encounter the curses. What will the Israelites do next?

2. What does God promise to do for them in response?

3. In 31:6–8 and 31:23, Moses and the LORD tell Joshua to be strong and not fearful. What do they give as the reason behind Joshua's strength and courage?

4. According to 31:17, what reason will the Israelites list for their troubles?

5. According to 31:20, are the Israelites more inclined to rebel in times of trouble or in times of blessing?

DAY 81 / DEUTERONOMY 32–34; PSALM 91

1. Look up "Jeshurun" (32:15) in a Hebrew lexicon and write down what you find.

2. What does 32:17 imply about false gods?

3. What does God promise to do in 32:21?

4. Read Romans 10:19 and 11:11–14. How does this show a fulfillment of God's promise in 32:21?

5. What does God list in 32:51 as the reason Moses doesn't get to enter the promised land? How does this correspond to the reason Moses listed earlier in 1:37, 3:26, and 4:21?

6. What two images does Moses use to describe the LORD in 33:29? How are these fitting complements to each other?

DAY 82 / JOSHUA 1–4

1. Who wrote Joshua?

2. To or for whom was it written?

3. When was it written?

4. What is the literary style (narrative, history, wisdom, prophecy, letter, etc.)?

5. Rahab lies to the king's men. Why doesn't God punish her dishonesty?

6. Read Hebrews 11:31, James 2:25, and Matthew 1:5–6. What role does Rahab play in God's ultimate plan?

7. When does God part the Jordan River (3:12–16)? Review Exodus 14:21–22. How is this different from when they crossed the Red Sea? What might these distinctions imply?

8. What day do they enter the promised land (4:19)? Review Exodus 12:1–3. Why is this timing significant?

DAY 83 / JOSHUA 5–8

1. God sent them manna in the wilderness for forty years, and He even sends them manna in the promised land. What day does He stop sending the manna (5:10–12)? What does this reveal about His character?

2. What clues do we see in 5:13–15 that the commander of the LORD's army is God Himself?

3. There are several unconventional aspects to the military strategy God employs in 6:1–21. Which ones stood out to you most?

4. Look up the phrase "broke faith" (7:1) in a Hebrew lexicon and write down what you find. (*Gesenius' Hebrew-Chaldee Lexicon* on blueletterbible.org is especially helpful here.)

5. Is there anything sinful about the specific items Achan takes in 7:20–21? What is the root of the problem in this situation?

DAY 84 / JOSHUA 9–11

1. Where does Israel go wrong in their response to the Gibeonites (or Hivites)?

2. When Joshua realizes he has been deceived, how does he respond?

3. The battle against the five Amorite kings is really Gibeon's battle. Why does Joshua intervene?

4. What three unique tactics does God employ in the battle against the five Amorite kings (10:8–14)?

5. In 10:19, Joshua tells his men how to proceed against their enemies and promises that God has given their enemies into their hands. How does he know?

DAY 85 / JOSHUA 12–15

1. Visual search: Locate Israel on a world map. It serves as a gateway between three continents. Which continents are they?

2. Visual search: Find a map of the tribal allotments for ancient Israel. How many tribes are in the Transjordan (on the east side of the Jordan River)? How many tribes are in the promised land?

3. Which tribe has land in both the Transjordan and the promised land?

4. Which tribe has no land allotment? Why?

5. In today's reading, which person gets to choose where they live? Why?

6. Look up the word "Negev" (15:19), or "Negeb," and write down what you find. What is the regional climate?

7. What does Achsah ask her father, Caleb, for? In light of question 6, why is this a wise thing for her to request?

DAY 86 / JOSHUA 16–18

1. Joseph is one of the twelve tribes of Israel (sons of Jacob), but he has no land allotment. Instead, his land is given to his two sons. What are their names?

2. How do we see Manasseh hedging on obedience in 17:12–13?

3. Which tribes complain about their land allotment? Why? How is their entitlement connected to their disobedience?

4. In what city is the tabernacle set up? Which tribal allotment has possession of this city?

DAY 87 / JOSHUA 19–21

1. One tribe's inheritance falls in the middle of another tribe's inheritance. Name both tribes.

2. Which tribe loses their inheritance and relocates?

3. In today's reading, which person gets to choose where they live? Why?

4. What land does he choose? Is it within his tribe's allotment?

5. How long does a manslayer have to live in the city of refuge?

DAY 88 / JOSHUA 22–24

1. What do the western tribes (in the original promised land) think the Transjordan tribes are doing when they build something at the border? How would this defy God and His commands?

2. Who heads up the team of people to go address the problem? What else is he known for (see Numbers 25:7–15)?

3. What are the Transjordan tribes actually aiming to do? How does this honor God?

4. As Joshua's life comes to a close, he reiterates one of the chief messages Moses repeated before his own death. What is it?

5. Review Genesis 50:25. Where do we see this promise fulfilled today? Approximately how long did it take for the fulfillment to happen?

DAY 89 / JUDGES 1–2

1. Who wrote Judges?

2. To or for whom was it written?

3. When was it written?

4. What is the literary style (narrative, history, wisdom, prophecy, letter, etc.)?

5. Which people group does the tribe of Benjamin fail to drive out of their land? Where do those people live?

6. What do most of the other tribes do to the Canaanites in their land, instead of driving them out as God had commanded?

7. What clues do we see in 2:1–3 that the Angel of the LORD is God Himself?

8. Review Numbers 33:50–56 and Joshua 23:11–13. How do we see this promise coming to fulfillment in today's reading?

DAY 90 / JUDGES 3–5

1. Review 3:7–9 and 3:12–15. Identify the pattern established in these two stories. How would you break this pattern down and summarize its separate phases?

2. Look up the word "Benjamite" (3:15) in a Hebrew lexicon. Write down what the word means.

3. Where does Sisera run when he escapes in battle? Why?

4. How is Deborah's prophecy from 4:9 fulfilled?

5. In the Song of Deborah and Barak, ten of the twelve tribes are referenced. (Note: "Machir" in 5:14 refers to West Manasseh. "Gilead" in 5:17 refers to East Manasseh.) Which tribes aren't mentioned at all? Which tribes are rebuked or questioned in the song for not participating in Israel's battle?

DAY 91 / JUDGES 6–7

1. The Midianites are oppressing the Israelites (6:1). Who are they in relationship to the Israelites? What has this relationship looked like through the years? (Review Genesis 25:1–2, 37:28; Exodus 3:1; and Numbers 25:16–18, 31:7 for help if you need it.)

2. Instead of sending a judge in the form of a military leader like He has in the past, God sends a different kind of leader this time. What type of leader does He send instead (6:7–8)? What do you think motivated a shift like this?

3. What clues do we see in the text that the Angel of the Lord is God Himself (6:11–27)?

4. How many men does Gideon's army start out with? How many are left in the army after God's reductions? Why would God want to reduce the size of Gideon's army?

5. What "weapons" do Gideon's men use in the battle?

6. How would you describe Gideon's attitude(s) and actions in today's reading?

DAY 92 / JUDGES 8–9

1. Why is the tribe of Ephraim angry with Gideon? What seems to be the root of that anger?

2. What two towns reject Gideon and his army? What does he do in retaliation? Is this God-directed or Gideon-directed?

3. Who is Jerubbaal? (See 6:32 and 7:1 for help.)

4. Look up the name "Abimelech" (8:31) in a Hebrew lexicon. What does the name mean?

5. How would you describe Gideon's attitude(s) and actions in to-day's reading? What has shifted since yesterday's reading?

6. How would you describe Abimelech's attitude(s) and actions in today's reading?

DAY 93 / JUDGES 10–12

1. List the gods that Israel follows instead of YHWH, according to 10:6.

2. In the early chapters of Judges, God responded by sending military leaders and prophets as judges to lead Israel when they cried out to Him for help. Summarize the way God responds to their cries in 10:10–14.

3. When they're threatened by the Ammonites and need a military leader, who do the Israelites consult for guidance on the decision (10:17–18)? Who do they end up appointing?

4. Jephthah makes a rash vow to God. Review Leviticus 5:4–6 and Deuteronomy 18:10. What options does he have based on what happens when he returns home? Is he right in what he says in 11:35?

5. Why is the tribe of Ephraim angry in 12:1–2? Is their anger justified? What do they do as a result of their anger?

DAY 94 / JUDGES 13–15

1. What clues do we see in the text that the Angel of the LORD could be God Himself?

2. Describe Samson. How would you summarize his attitudes and actions from today's reading?

3. Where does Samson get his strength to accomplish such amazing feats? (See 14:6, 14:19, and 15:14 for help.)

4. Review 13:4 and Numbers 6:1–6. How is Samson disobeying his vow in 14:8–9 and 15:15?

5. Why does Samson's wife press him to tell her the answer to the riddle?

DAY 95 / JUDGES 16–18

1. Yesterday we saw that Samson's strength came from the presence of God's Spirit. Where does Samson mistakenly think it comes from?

2. Does Delilah love Samson in return? Why does she enter into a relationship with him? How is this similar to what happened with his wife?

3. Review 17:2, 5, and 13. What does Micah seem to be after? On the surface, how might this look different?

4. Read Judges 1:34 and Joshua 19:47–48. Why are the Danites looking for a new place to live?

5. Review 18:25–30. Describe the Danites. How would you summarize their attitudes and actions?

DAY 96 / JUDGES 19–21

1. In what city and tribe do the Levite, his concubine, and his servant spend the night?

2. Who are the men who show up with wicked requests? (See 20:5 for help.)

3. How do the Benjamites respond when confronted with the evil actions of their leaders?

4. In all of today's reading, there was no mention of consulting God except in chapter 20 (20:18, 23, and 27–28). What does God endorse in this passage? Why? What does that reveal about Him?

5. In 21:25, the book ends with a reminder of why all these evil things have happened. Based on this information, are these stories descriptive or prescriptive? Do they describe what happened (descriptive) or are they telling us how to live (prescriptive)?

DAY 97 / RUTH 1–4

1. Who wrote Ruth?

2. To or for whom was it written?

3. When was it written?

4. What is the literary style (narrative, history, wisdom, prophecy, letter, etc.)?

5. Which person in this story seems to struggle most with trusting in God and finding joy in Him? Which person never seems to doubt God?

6. Does the presence of doubt, despair, hope, or faith alter God's blessings to those people (see question 5 above)? Does He treat them differently?

DAY 98 / 1 SAMUEL 1–3

1. Who wrote 1 Samuel?

2. To or for whom was it written?

3. When was it written?

4. What is the literary style (narrative, history, wisdom, prophecy, letter, etc.)?

5. Which tribe do Hannah and Elkanah belong to? And which tribe are they assigned to live with?

6. What does Hannah reveal about God by entering the tabernacle and taking her pain to Him?

7. Did you see any prophecies of Jesus in today's reading?

8. Why do you think Samuel doesn't recognize God's voice?

DAY 99 / 1 SAMUEL 4–8

1. Which piece of bad news is most devastating to Eli? Why might this be the case?

2. Why would milk cows be a good option for the Philistines' experiment to see if God is causing their plagues?

3. Review Leviticus 1:3 and Numbers 4:5–6. Which laws do the Israelites break when they regain the ark of the covenant?

4. Look up the word "Ebenezer" (7:12) in a Hebrew lexicon. What does the name mean?

5. By asking for a king, which leader over them have the Israelites rejected?

DAY 100 / 1 SAMUEL 9–12

1. Which tribe does Saul belong to? What recent event did this tribe participate in? How are they viewed by other Israelites at this time?

2. Where does Samuel tell Saul to meet him? And how long does he say to wait for him there?

3. What evidence does Samuel give to Saul to help him believe his words are truly from God?

4. What produces a change in Saul? Is the change permanent? Why or why not?

5. When God reveals the people's sin to them, how do they respond? With what attributes of God's character does Samuel encourage them?

DAY 101 / 1 SAMUEL 13–14

1. Review 10:8. How long is Saul supposed to wait for Samuel? Is he supposed to act alone?

2. What does Saul do when confronted with his rebellious actions?

3. What consequence does God (via Samuel) hand out to Saul in response to his sin?

4. What does the phrase "a man after His own heart" (13:14) mean? Use a study Bible for help.

5. Describe Jonathan. How would you summarize his attitude and actions?

6. Why do you think God doesn't immediately answer Saul's request for guidance in 14:37?

DAY 102 / 1 SAMUEL 15–17

1. Review 15:3, Exodus 17:14, and Deuteronomy 25:19. What does God call the Israelites to do?

2. List the types of lies Saul tells in response to Samuel's confrontation.

3. Review 15:11 and 15:29. How is it possible that these two verses don't contradict each other? For help, look up the word "regret" (15:11) in a Hebrew lexicon. Use biblehub.com to see other possible translations of 15:11 that might fit the context.

4. When Samuel privately anoints David as king, what does God the Spirit do?

5. In 17:28–29, what do you think is really underneath Eliab's anger toward David?

DAY 103 / 1 SAMUEL 18–20; PSALMS 11, 59

1. Look up the word "primogeniture" in a dictionary and write down what you find.

2. List the instances you can recall from Scripture where God overturned primogeniture.

3. According to 18:12, why does Saul fear David? How do you think Saul knows this?

4. What promise does Jonathan ask David to make in 20:15?

5. Review Psalm 59:8. Then read Psalm 2:4 and 37:12. These are the only times Scripture records God's laughter. What do these instances have in common? What does this reveal about God?

DAY 104 / 1 SAMUEL 21–24

1. According to 22:1–2, what type of men are the first men under David's leadership? What do you think he learns through this experience that equips him to be a better king?

2. Saul is seeking after his "heart's desire" (23:20). What does this reveal about the folly of following our own hearts?

3. David, on the other hand, follows something else. What is it? (See 23:2, 4, and 10–12.)

4. What promise does David make to Saul in 24:21? What does this reveal about David's character?

5. Read Matthew 10:16. List all the ways David demonstrates these types of behavior in today's reading.

DAY 105 / PSALMS 7, 27, 31, 34, 52

1. In Psalm 7, who does David suggest should be punished if he is innocent? Why? How does this request align with God's character?

2. In 31:10, what iniquity might David be referring to?

3. According to Psalm 34:4, what does looking to God deliver us from? Compare this to 34:19. How do these two verses work together?

4. What aspects of God's character does David emphasize in Psalm 52?

5. Did you see any prophecies of Jesus in today's reading? If so, what are they and where are they fulfilled?

DAY 106 / PSALMS 56, 120, 140–142

1. In chapter 56, what poetic imagery does David use to describe God's nearness and attention to him in the midst of his trials?

2. How do David's cries for vengeance in Psalm 140 appeal to God's character and what He values?

3. In Psalm 141:3–4, list the areas of David's life that he asks God to direct in righteous ways.

4. In Psalm 142:1–2, how does David display the intimacy of his relationship with God?

1. Describe Abigail. How would you summarize her attitude and actions in today's reading?

2. Abigail knows a lot about David. What facts about his past and his future does she reference?

3. Compare David's initial response to Nabal with David's responses to Saul through the years. Why do you think his response to Nabal is so different?

4. David tells Saul to consider what has motivated him to chase him down. What two options does he suggest might be the source of Saul's actions? Which option is accurate?

5. Review 27:1. Describe what is happening in David's heart and mind. Where has he gone wrong in this? What do these fears and feelings lead him to do?

DAY 108 / PSALMS 17, 35, 54, 63

1. In Psalm 17:1, David claims his lips are free from deceit. What do you think David is pointing toward? Is he claiming total innocence?

2. In 35:6, who does David ask God to send to his rescue?

3. In chapter 35, David asks God to pursue vengeance against his enemies, but how does he treat them personally? Is this hypocritical or dishonest on his part? Why or why not?

4. In Psalm 63:1–3, how does David's prayer reflect his present location and his former location? Though his circumstances change dramatically between verses 1 and 2, what remains the same?

DAY 109 / 1 SAMUEL 28–31; PSALM 18

1. Why isn't God answering Saul's prayer? What does Saul do in response to God's silence? Does he know this is the wrong choice? Why or why not?

2. When Samuel appears to the medium, how does she respond? What does this suggest about this kind of occurrence?

3. Read 1 Chronicles 10:13–14. What does it reveal about today's series of events?

4. When the Philistines head to war and David goes with them, what opposition stops him in his tracks? How do you see God's kindness and provision on display in this story?

5. In 1 Samuel 30–31, what two battles are happening simultaneously? List out the parties involved.

6. How does 30:22 describe some of the men who fought alongside David in defeating the Amalekites? What does this reveal about the distinction between action and motive?

DAY 110 / PSALMS 121, 123–125, 128–130

1. In the pagan culture of David's day, the gods they worshipped had to be woken from their sleep by acts like human sacrifice and

cutting. Given that setting, why is 121:4 such a comforting thought for David and the Israelites?

2. Psalm 121 is a Song of Ascent, which the Israelites sang as they made their pilgrimages to Jerusalem three times each year. What other aspects of this chapter would be particularly comforting to someone traveling for weeks through the desert?

3. Psalm 124 and 125 poetically recount the blessings God has given them through the years. Which ones stand out most in your memory of their story?

4. What are some of the dangers of trying to "claim" promises like the ones in Psalm 128 for ourselves today? Is it frustrating to only see what it reveals about God's character without being able to "claim it" for yourself? If so, what does that reveal to you about what you're really after?

5. Rewrite Psalm 130:4 in your own words.

1. Who wrote 2 Samuel?

2. To or for whom was it written?

3. When was it written?

4. What is the literary style (narrative, history, wisdom, prophecy, letter, etc.)?

5. Who takes credit for Saul's death in today's reading? Review 1 Samuel 31:4. Who does Scripture say is responsible for Saul's death?

6. Israel's first king has just been killed in battle, and Israel's next king was anointed by Samuel—who is also dead—years earlier. According to 2:1–7, how does David approach stepping into that role? What is his process?

7. With David established as king over the tribe of Judah, who steps up to lead the remaining tribes of Israel (see 2:8–11)?

8. With two kings over God's people (one in Judah and one in Israel), which leader in the ranks unexpectedly switches his loyalty? What prompts this change? What is required of him in order to be approved by the other king (chapter 3)?

9. After all these deaths and murders, who is the only surviving member of Saul's family (4:4)?

DAY 112 / PSALMS 6, 8–10, 14, 16, 19, 21

1. Review 8:3–4. Why is mankind distinct among the rest of God's creation (see Genesis 1:26–27)?

2. What might it mean that humans are made "lower" than the heavenly beings in 8:5, especially considering 8:6? How could mankind be "lower"? Consider 1 Corinthians 6:13 and 1 Peter 1:12.

3. Review 14:1–3, then read Romans 3:10–12. How does this inform the way we think about humanity? Are humans born naturally good? Why or why not? Support your answer with Scripture.

4. Rewrite Psalm 16:11 in your own words.

5. Did you see any prophecies of Jesus in today's reading? If so, where are they fulfilled?

DAY 113 / 1 CHRONICLES 1–2

1. Who wrote 1 Chronicles?

2. To or for whom was it written?

3. When was it written?

4. What is the literary style (narrative, history, wisdom, prophecy, letter, etc.)?

5. What does 1:10 reveal about Nimrod? Review Genesis 10:8–12 for more info.

6. What does 1:19 reveal about Peleg? Review Genesis 10:25 for more info.

7. Why do you think chapter 2 focuses primarily on the line of Judah?

8. What does 2:7 reveal about Achan? Review Joshua 7 for more info.

DAY 114 / PSALMS 43–45, 49, 84–85, 87

1. David spends the first four verses of Psalm 43 talking to God. Who is he talking to in the last verse? What can we learn from this practice? Why is it important?

2. What does David do in the first three verses of Psalm 44? What can we learn from this practice? Why is it important?

3. According to Psalm 49, what do the foolish and the wise have in common? Why is it important to remember this?

4. Review Exodus 34:6–7 and write a list of the characteristics of God mentioned. Many (though not all) of these characteristics are referenced or described in Psalm 85. Beside each characteristic, write the verse number from Psalm 85 that addresses it.

5. Look up the name "Rahab" (87:4) in a Hebrew lexicon. What possible definitions are given? Which seems most likely?

DAY 115 / 1 CHRONICLES 3–5

1. Does Scripture's description of David's many wives indicate that God approves of this? What can we learn from Scripture's inclusion of details like this?

2. Do you see any parallels to Jesus in 3:4?

3. What can we learn about the character of Jabez (4:9–10) based on his prayer?

4. What do we learn about the tribe of Simeon in 4:27? Review Genesis 34:25–29 and 49:7 and Deuteronomy 33. What does this tell us about what's happening in 4:27?

5. Why did the tribe of Reuben (Jacob's firstborn son) lose their firstborn inheritance? To whom was it given, and which tribes are included in that?

1. Who is Asaph focused on in the first half of Psalm 73? How does this impact his thoughts and emotions?

2. What change does Asaph make to his perspective in 73:16–17? How does that shift impact his thoughts and emotions in the rest of the chapter?

3. In 77:6, Asaph says he is meditating in his heart. Based on verses 4–5, what is he meditating on? How does that impact his view in verses 7–9?

4. In 77:10, Asaph changes what he's meditating on. What does his focus shift onto? How does that shift impact his thoughts and emotions in the rest of the chapter?

5. Underline or record every use of these phrases or ideas in Psalm 78: "forgot," "did not remember," "did not keep," "did not believe." What is a consistent theme resulting from those phrases?

DAY 117 / 1 CHRONICLES 6

1. First Chronicles was written after the current events we're reading about. It records history after the fact. In 6:15, we get a sneak peek into something that will happen in the future. What is it?

2. Review Leviticus 26:14–17, Deuteronomy 28:49–52, and 1 Samuel 12:14–15. Based on what 6:15 says will happen in the future, what can we assume the Israelites will eventually do?

3. God says He'll bring them back to this land someday in the future, after their time in exile is over. Based on that promise, why would these genealogies be important for their return?

4. What new role does David establish for the service of the temple in 6:31–32?

DAY 118 / PSALMS 81, 88, 92–93

1. According to Psalm 81:15, how do God's enemies respond to Him?

2. How does Heman open Psalm 88? Given the content of his song, how is this a helpful introduction? Do any aspects of this psalm seem to contradict other things we know about God from Scripture?

3. According to Psalm 92:1–2, what is a good way to bookend our days?

4. In Psalm 92:7–9, the psalmist points out that the wicked are blessed. How does he describe them and their blessings?

DAY 119 / 1 CHRONICLES 7–10

1. The genealogies of chapter 7 list only one person who accomplishes a significant task. Who is this person and what is the accomplishment? Why is it noteworthy that it is listed?

2. In chapters 8–9, which tribe has two genealogies listed?

3. Chapter 9 records a future exile. Why are the people exiled?

4. Chapter 9 also records their future return after that exile ends. Which tribe is the first to return? What might be the reason for this?

5. According to chapter 10, which version of Saul's death is correct—the one Scripture recorded in 1 Samuel or the story the Amalekite sojourner told David in 2 Samuel 1:6–10?

DAY 120 / **PSALMS 102–104**

1. According to Psalm 102:9–10, to what does the psalmist attribute his pain?

2. What prompts God's anger?

3. Review Exodus 34:6–7. Compare it to Psalm 103:8–13 and write down the similarities you notice.

4. Psalm 104 is an ode to God's good plan for creation. What do verses 14 and 23 reveal to us about God's good plan for work?

1. In what city is David anointed king of Israel? Visual search: Locate that city on a map of ancient Israel.

2. To which city does David want to move the capital of Israel? Visual search: Locate that city on a map of ancient Israel.

3. What is David's biggest challenge with moving the capital to this new location? What threats do the people there make against him?

4. What trick does David use for taking the city?

5. David is accumulating wives and concubines (5:13). Is this descriptive or prescriptive? What did God have to say about this in Deuteronomy 17:17?

6. Look up the phrase "LORD of hosts" (11:9) in a Hebrew lexicon. Write down what you find.

DAY 122 / PSALM 133

1. Review Genesis 13:6 and 36:7. Name both pairs of people represented in these two verses. What theme shows up in both verses?

2. How does 133:1 connect us back to those scenarios from Genesis? Which is better—the Genesis scenario or the Psalms scenario?

3. What is the elevation of Mount Hermon? Visual search: Locate Mount Hermon on a map of Israel. Then look up an image of Mount Hermon.

4. What is the elevation of Mount Zion? Visual search: Locate Mount Zion on a map of Israel. Then look up an image of Mount Zion.

5. Given the elevation of each mountain and the terrain and distance between them, is it possible that the dew from Mount Hermon would impact Mount Zion? What can we learn about unity in God's family based on this imagery from David?

6. What kind of blessing does God command on the land?

7. Given the division of Judah and Israel that David emerged from when he became king of all Israel, how is this psalm a fitting song of praise?

DAY 123 / PSALMS 106–107

1. According to 106:8, why did God save His rebellious people? According to 106:45, why did God save His rebellious people? How do these two varying statements work in tandem?

2. What did the ancient Israelites forget in Psalm 106:7 that impacted the way they lived?

3. How does Moses display Christ to us in 106:23?

4. List the four types of people who are in trouble in Psalm 107 (vv. 4–9, 10–16, 17–22, 23–26). Beside each type of person, write the reason for their trouble.

5. What is challenging about wandering in "trackless wastes" (107:40)? Why is that a form of punishment or discipline?

DAY 124 / 1 CHRONICLES 13–16

1. Where is the ark of the covenant at the start of today's reading? Why is it there? (Review 1 Samuel 6:1–7:2 for help.) How long has it been there?

2. Review Exodus 25:10–15 and Numbers 4:15. What rules has God given for how the ark of the covenant should be transported?

3. Who previously broke this rule and what did they use? (Review 1 Samuel 6:1–9 for help.)

4. How does David carry the cart in 13:7?

5. Where does David send the ark after tragedy occurs?

6. In 15:1–15, David displays his repentance before resuming the effort to bring the ark to Jerusalem. Who does he list as being guilty alongside him in the previous failed attempt? Is he correct in this? Why or why not?

DAY 125 / PSALMS 1–2, 15, 22–24, 47, 68

1. Who is God laughing at in 2:4? Why? What does this reveal about God and His character?

2. In Psalm 2:7–9, the psalmist is quoting the words of God. Who was God originally speaking to in this quote? To whom else does this quote point? See 2 Samuel 7:14–16 for help. (Hint: Neither of the answers is "us" or "me.")

3. What does it mean to "beget" something, as in "today I have begotten you" (2:7)? David wasn't conceived or born on the day God spoke these words to him, so what other definitions could apply? Use a dictionary or a Hebrew lexicon for help.

4. In Psalm 22, review verses 1 and 24. The two verses seem to contradict each other at first glance. Which verse states a feeling, and which verse states a fact?

5. According to Psalm 24:5, what are three things we receive from the LORD? What does this reveal to us about God and His character? What does it reveal to us about ourselves in light of Him?

DAY 126 / PSALMS 89, 96, 100–101, 105, 132

1. In Psalm 89, review verses 30–32 and verses 38–45. One states the cause, and the other states the psalmist's feelings in response to the cause. Which is which? Given what we know about God, what can we assume about the psalmist's feelings?

2. How does the psalmist end Psalm 89? What does it reveal about God that the psalmist feels free to bring his emotions and frustrations to God while also blessing and praising Him?

3. Look up the word "idols" (96:5) in a Hebrew lexicon and write down what you find. What does this reveal about "the gods of the peoples"?

4. How would you describe the kind of man David is aiming to be in Psalm 101? How does he begin to move in this direction, according to verse 1?

DAY 127 / 2 SAMUEL 6–7; 1 CHRONICLES 17

1. According to Scripture, what is David wearing when he enters the city with the ark? How does Michal describe his attire? Which description suggests fact and which suggests feeling?

2. What does David want to do for God in chapter 7? What is the prophet Nathan's first counsel to him? What is Nathan's second counsel to him? Why does Nathan's counsel change?

3. How does God describe David's desire? What is God's answer to David's desire?

4. What promises does God make to David instead of giving David what he wants?

5. What does God's "no" to David's good desire reveal to us about God and His character? What does it reveal to us about ourselves in light of Him?

DAY 128 / PSALMS 25, 29, 33, 36, 39

1. According to Psalm 25:6–7, what three things does David ask God to remember? What two things does David ask God to forget? And why?

2. In Psalm 25, review verses 9 and 12. What two descriptors does David give of the type of person God leads, teaches, and instructs? How do these two descriptors overlap? Why is it hard to lead, teach, and instruct someone who doesn't possess these traits?

3. Using two or three words, how would you summarize David's descriptions of God and His actions in Psalm 29:3–10? Then review verse 11. How do these two ideas work together?

4. Psalm 36 is broken into four sections: verses 1–4, 5–6, 7–9, and 10–12. Write a sentence summarizing the content of each section. Which section resonates with you most and why?

5. Look up "discipline" and "rebukes" (39:11) in a Hebrew lexicon and write what you find.

DAY 129 / 2 SAMUEL 8–9; 1 CHRONICLES 18

1. In 2 Samuel 8, what does God give to David? What does David "give" (dedicate) back to God?

2. According to 1 Chronicles 18:8, what are the items David dedicated to God used for?

3. What does David's question in 2 Samuel 9:1 reveal about his character? Review 1 Samuel 20:12–17 for help.

4. What picture of Christ do we see in the story of David and Mephibosheth?

1. God testifies against Israel in 50:7–13. What is it that He says He doesn't need from them? Is this surprising? Why or why not?

2. According to 50:14–23, what is it that He really wants from them? (See Hosea 6:6, 1 Samuel 15:22, and Psalm 51:16–17 for help.) While both still involve sacrifices, what makes the distinction between these two types of offerings?

3. Review 60:3 and 75:8. What does wine represent in this repeated metaphor?

4. What do the regions in 60:7 have in common? What kind of position(s) does God give them?

5. What do the regions in 60:8 have in common? What kind of position(s) does God give them?

DAY 131 / 2 SAMUEL 10; 1 CHRONICLES 19; PSALM 20

1. Why does David send servants to King Hanun of the Ammonites? How does this act of kindness backfire?

2. When the Ammonites go to war against Israel, who do they hire to help them fight the battle?

3. Who are the two leaders of the two divisions of Israel's army?

4. How would you summarize Joab's counsel to Abishai before the battle (10:12)?

5. What ends up happening to the Syrian mercenaries after round two of the battle (10:15–19)?

DAY 132 / PSALMS 65–67, 69–70

1. David wrote Psalm 65 hundreds of years before Jesus was born. How could he have known the truth of verse 3?

2. According to 66:3, what type of person approaches God with the negative type of fear? How is this different from the mind-set and relationship that come from the positive type of fear?

3. Look up the word "listened" (66:18) in a Hebrew lexicon and write what you find. What other possible definitions might fit the context here?

4. In Psalm 67, the psalmist makes at least nine separate mentions of the people he wants to know and praise God. Who are these people? Write down each reference.

5. What prophecies and foreshadowing of Jesus do you see in Psalm 69?

1. How does 11:1 describe springtime? According to 11:1, what does David do during this time? What does this suggest about his leadership and character?

2. Who is Uriah, according to 11:3? Review 1 Chronicles 11:10 and 41. What else do we learn about Uriah from these verses?

3. According to 2 Samuel 11:27, whom is God displeased with?

4. When God sends Nathan to confront David about his sins, how does David initially respond?

5. According to 2 Samuel 12:13, what has God done with David's sin?

6. According to 12:6, how many lambs must be restored for the one killed? According to 12:10–14, how many consequences will there be for David's sins? What are the consequences?

DAY 134 / PSALMS 32, 51, 86, 122

1. According to 32:1, what blessings does God give us when we sin?

2. What's causing David to feel the heaviness he describes in 32:3–5?

3. According to 51:5, how long has David been a sinner?

4. In 51:11, what does David ask God not to do? Why was this a fitting prayer in David's time? Why is it not a fitting prayer today? (See John 14:16, Romans 8:9, Ephesians 1:13–14, 2 Corinthians 1:22, and Ephesians 4:30 for help.)

5. According to 86:9, which nations will praise God? Why is it significant that the king of Israel is making this claim?

1. According to Deuteronomy 22:25–27, what does the law require of Amnon in response to his sin against Tamar? And at the very least, what does the law require him to offer her and her family, according to Exodus 22:16–17?

2. How does Amnon repeat the sins of his father, David?

3. How does Absalom repeat the sins of his father, David, in chapter 13 specifically?

4. Review the four consequences of David's sin from 2 Samuel 12:10–14. Which one had already occurred before the start of today's reading (review 2 Samuel 12:15–23)? Which one occurs in today's reading?

5. Ahithophel is David's advisor, but he betrays him and turns to advise Absalom instead. Read 2 Samuel 23:34 and 11:3. Based on these verses, what do you think might be prompting Ahithophel's betrayal of David?

DAY 136 / PSALMS 3–4, 12–13, 28, 55

1. According to Psalm 3:2, what are David's enemies saying about him? Are they right or wrong? How do you know? (Cite Scripture if you can.)

2. In 4:4–5, David gives advice about how to handle anger righteously so that it doesn't lead to sin. Write out his counsel in your own words. Which aspect of this is hardest for you?

3. What relationship is emphasized five times in 28:8–9? Write out each unique way David references this relationship. Which of these references resonates with you the most? Why?

4. How does David's prayer in Psalm 55:9 mirror his prayer from yesterday in 2 Samuel 15:31? What does this prayer reveal to us about God and His character?

DAY 137 / 2 SAMUEL 16–18

1. When Ziba meets David, what information does he relay about Mephibosheth?

2. What does Shimei accuse David of doing? Is he right or wrong?

3. Summarize David's response to Shimei's attack. How would you characterize this response? What does it reveal about God and His character that David can respond like this?

4. According to Absalom in 17:14, why doesn't he choose to follow Ahithophel's advice? Is Absalom right or wrong?

5. How does Joab defy David's command in chapter 18?

DAY 138 / PSALMS 26, 40, 58, 61–62, 64

1. According to 26:5, what kind of company does David aim to keep? How is this statement ironic in light of what is happening in his life at the time?

2. Look up the word "gods" (58:1) in a Hebrew lexicon and write down what you find.

3. Based on what you found in prompt 2, who is David's anger directed toward in Psalm 58?

4. Read Psalm 63:6–7 and compare it to 40:1–3 and 61:3. What spiritual discipline is David practicing in these passages?

5. How is that practice different from the spiritual discipline he describes in 40:9–10?

DAY 139 / 2 SAMUEL 19–21

1. Review 2 Samuel 16:1–4. Who is Ziba? According to David's encounter with Mephibosheth today in 19:24–30, was Ziba telling the truth in 16:1–4? Summarize David's response to this situation.

2. Review 2 Samuel 16:5–14. Who is Shimei? How does he respond to David today in 19:16–23?

3. What promise does David make to Shimei?

4. How would you summarize the actions and the character of the "wise woman" in 20:14–22?

5. In chapter 21, why is the land suffering a famine? What does this reveal about God and His character as it pertains to His covenant with Israel?

DAY 140 / PSALMS 5, 38, 41–42

1. According to Psalm 5, why is David allowed to enter God's house?

2. Why does David want God to punish his enemies in Psalm 5? How does this correspond to God's character?

3. David is suffering on lots of levels in Psalm 38. Briefly list the various kinds of trouble he's enduring. In the midst of all these types of trouble, what kind of relief does David ask God for?

4. According to Psalm 41, what kind of person is blessed, or happy? Knowing what you know about God and His character, why do you think this is someone God blesses?

DAY 141 / 2 SAMUEL 22–23; PSALM 57

1. Find every action verb attributed to God in chapter 22. Either circle it in your Bible or list it here.

2. How can David make the claims he makes in 22:21–25?

3. According to David's song in chapter 22, what aspect of God's character does David say is responsible for his own advancement?

4. Look up the phrase "worthless men" (23:6) in a Hebrew lexicon and write down what you find.

5. What was David's motive in refusing the water brought by three of his mighty men (23:13–17)?

DAY 142 / PSALMS 95, 97–99

1. How would you summarize the psalmist's description of God in 95:3–5?

2. What three acts or postures are described in Psalm 95:6? Look up each of those three words in a Hebrew lexicon and write down what you find.

3. How would you summarize the psalmist's description of God in 95:7? Compare and contrast this with the description in 95:3–5. What do the two separate descriptions display to us about God?

4. What does the psalmist call us to do in 97:10? Given that "God is love," is this a challenging idea for you? Why or why not?

5. How would you summarize or explain the two ideas the psalmist expresses in 99:8?

1. According to 2 Samuel 24, who incites David to take the census? According to 1 Chronicles 21, who incites David to take the census? How could these two accounts work together?

2. In the past, God has commanded the leaders to take a census. Why is this particular census an act of sin on David's part? Use a study Bible for help.

3. What are David's three options for his consequence? Which does he choose? Which would you choose?

4. What prompts the Angel of the LORD to halt His acts of justice?

5. Where does God command David to offer his sacrifice? Why is this a terrifying challenge for David?

6. Read 2 Chronicles 3:1. In what city and on what mountain is this threshing floor located? Now read Genesis 22:1–3. What other sacrifice was provided on that mountain?

DAY 144 / PSALMS 108–110

1. According to Psalm 109:4, what does David do when his enemies accuse him?

2. David wants his enemies to get justice. How does he go about making sure this happens?

3. Knowing what we know about "Lord" versus "Lord," and given that David is the one writing Psalm 110 in a first-person account, who are the two people he is referring to in Psalm 110:1?

4. Do you see any prophecies of Jesus in Psalm 110? If so, where are they fulfilled?

DAY 145 / 1 CHRONICLES 23–25

1. What is the minimum age limit for a priest who can serve in the temple?

2. How many Levites fit that requirement?

3. What are the three family divisions David uses in dividing the Levites into their roles?

4. In chapter 25, David also organizes a bonus group to serve in the temple. What is their unique role? How many are there (25:7), and how does this correspond to 23:5?

DAY 146 / PSALMS 131, 138–139, 143–145

1. In Psalm 131, how does David calm and quiet his soul?

2. Look up the word "gods" (138:1) in a Hebrew lexicon and write down what you find. Given the context, which definition seems most likely to you?

3. Find every action verb attributed to God in Psalm 139. Either circle it in your Bible or list it here.

4. Rewrite Psalm 139:23–24 in your own words here, then pray it aloud.

DAY 147 / 1 CHRONICLES 26–29; PSALM 127

1. According to 26:17–19, which gate (not including the road and colonnade) has the most guards?

2. When David took a census of the men, why would he only need to count the men over age twenty (27:23–24)?

3. What does 27:23–24 reveal to us about David's prior sin and motivations in 2 Samuel 24:1–10?

4. David and the people give a lot of wealth to help Solomon build the temple. Summarize David's words about these generous donations in 29:14–17.

5. How does Psalm 127:1 point back to two specific things we read about in the final chapters of 1 Chronicles today? What does this verse reveal about Solomon's heart and God's power?

DAY 148 / PSALMS 111–118

1. In 111:10, what do you think it means to "practice" the fear of the LORD?

2. Describe God's position according to 114:4–6. How does His position shift in 114:7–8? What does this point to or foreshadow?

3. Psalm 115 contrasts YHWH with the false gods of the pagan nations surrounding Israel. Summarize the description of YHWH (v. 3), then summarize that of the pagan gods (vv. 4–7).

4. Explain 116:15 in your own words. Does this verse feel challenging or encouraging? Why?

5. Read Matthew 21:1–11. Look up the word "hosanna" (21:9) in a Greek lexicon and write down what it means. Strong's lexicon is particularly helpful. Then read Matthew 21:42. Cite at least three

things in these stories from Palm Sunday that overlap with today's reading in Psalm 118:19–29.

DAY 149 / 1 KINGS 1–2; PSALMS 37, 71, 94

1. Who wrote 1 Kings?

2. To or for whom was it written?

3. When was it written?

4. What is the literary style (narrative, history, wisdom, prophecy, letter, etc.)?

5. Who does Adonijah fail to invite to his public sacrifice? Why do you think he chose to leave them out of the plan?

6. On his deathbed, David gives Solomon one word of counsel, followed by two specific commands. Summarize each of these three things.

7. Review 2 Samuel 19:23. Does this conflict with David's deathbed commands? Why or why not?

8. Write out two different possible interpretations for Psalm 37:4.

DAY 150 / PSALM 119

1. Most of the verses of this psalm have a connection back to God's Word and His law. Review verses 18, 27, 32, and 36. What other thing do each of the psalmist's requests have in common?

2. What unique thing does the psalmist thank God for in verses 71 and 75? Why?

3. Look up the word "lamp" (119:105) in a Hebrew lexicon and write what you find. Strong's lexicon is especially helpful.

4. Look up the word "light" (119:105) in a Hebrew lexicon and write what you find. Strong's lexicon is especially helpful.

5. How do those two similar words ("lamp," "light") demonstrate the very different roles God's Word plays in our lives?

DAY 151 / 1 KINGS 3–4

1. Why does Solomon marry his wife in 3:1? Is this a good reason? Why or why not? What does this kind of marriage indicate about Solomon's faith in God?

2. Describe Solomon's relationship with God at the time of 3:3–4.

3. What is Solomon doing when God asks him to make his request?

4. What does God promise to give Solomon in response to his request for wisdom?

5. Read James 1:5. What does God promise to give you if you ask for it? Write out a brief prayer asking God for this.

DAY 152 / 2 CHRONICLES 1; PSALM 72

1. Who wrote 2 Chronicles?

2. To or for whom was it written?

3. When was it written?

4. What is the literary style (narrative, history, wisdom, prophecy, letter, etc.)?

5. In today's account of Solomon's request for wisdom, God praises him for not requesting something. What is it? What does this reveal about God and His heart?

DAY 153 / SONG OF SOLOMON 1–8

1. Who wrote Song of Solomon?

2. To or for whom was it written?

3. When was it written?

4. What is the literary style (narrative, history, wisdom, prophecy, letter, etc.)?

5. If this book is a story about human love, what is one piece of wisdom we can glean from it?

6. If this book is an allegory about God's love for His people, what's something it reveals to us about God and His character?

DAY 154 / PROVERBS 1–3

1. Who wrote Proverbs?

2. To or for whom was it written?

3. When was it written?

4. What is the literary style (narrative, history, wisdom, prophecy, letter, etc.)?

5. List all the things the father tells his son to acquire in 2:1–5.

6. According to 2:6–8, where will the son find these things?

DAY 155 / PROVERBS 4–6

1. Review 4:14–16. List the six ways the father tells his son to respond to the path of the wicked.

2. Review 4:20–22. Based on these verses, what do you think the father means by his advice in the next verse (4:23)?

3. Review 5:6. How would you describe the adulterer's mind-set?

4. We hate things that violate what we love. According to this list of seven things that are an abomination to God and that He hates (6:16–19), write a list of seven things God loves.

DAY 156 / PROVERBS 7–9

1. According to 7:2–3, what three places does the father want his son to keep his commands? How would those three places in particular serve to impact and guide the son?

2. In 8:13, we see that the fear of the LORD prompts us toward a specific kind of hatred. What kind of hatred does it prompt in us?

3. In 8:12–21, we see a list of at least ten things that wisdom offers as benefits to those who pursue "her." List all the benefits you can find.

4. Based on 8:18, wisdom promises "enduring wealth." What do you think the author intends by using this phrase? What kind of wealth endures?

5. Which aspects of wisdom's benefits have you seen show up in your own life?

DAY 157 / **PROVERBS 10–12**

1. Rewrite 10:19 in your own words.

2. Review 10:8, 10:17, and 11:14. How would you summarize the message of these three verses?

3. What theme shows up in chapter 10, specifically in verses 11, 13, 14, 18–21, and 31–32? What aspect of this is most convicting to you?

4. Review 10:15, then compare it to 11:28. These two verses seem to contradict each other. How could they both be in Proverbs, written by the same author?

5. Pick a proverb from chapter 12 that represents an area where you desire to grow, and write it here in your own words, as a prayer to God:

DAY 158 / **PROVERBS 13–15**

1. Review 13:20. List three to five wise people in your life that you spend time with or want to spend more time with.

2. What theme(s) do you notice in 14:15, 14:16, and 14:29?

3. Rewrite 14:30 in your own words.

4. Read 1 Samuel 15:22 and Psalm 51:16–17. Then review 15:18. What does this reveal about what God is after? How does God feel when we check the "good deeds" box on our to-do list?

DAY 159 / **PROVERBS 16–18**

1. According to 16:20, you should discover something good in today's reading. What is the best thing you saw in these chapters? Write the verse or reference here:

2. Review 16:1 and 16:9. What theme do these two verses have in common?

3. Rewrite 17:24 in your own words.

4. What does 18:10 mean by "the name of the LORD"? How do you run to a name?

DAY 160 / PROVERBS 19–21

1. Review Proverbs 19:3. Do you tend to blame God for the consequences of your actions or the sins of others? Why or why not? What do you think is underneath that response?

2. What theme do you notice in 19:11, 20:3, and 21:9? What does 20:22 offer up as an alternative?

3. In Proverbs 19:17, with whom does God identify Himself? What does this reveal to us about His character?

4. In verses 19:13, 21:9, and 21:19, Solomon gives some undesirable traits in a spouse. List them. Then, considering that information, what traits would be desirable in a spouse?

5. What theme do you notice in 19:21, 20:24, and 21:1? Which three areas of life do the proverbs point to with this theme?

DAY 161 / PROVERBS 22–24

1. Review 22:5. What things or situations tend to act as thorns and snares for you? As you aim to walk in wisdom, how can you guard your soul by keeping far from them?

2. Review 24:3–4, then define the following terms (use a dictionary for help): "wisdom," "understanding," "knowledge."

3. How do these three words work together?

4. How would you summarize Solomon's message in 24:30–34?

DAY 162 / 1 KINGS 5–6; 2 CHRONICLES 2–3

1. According to 6:1, how much time passed between the Israelites being rescued out of Egyptian slavery and the temple being built in the promised land?

2. A cubit is approximately eighteen inches (one and a half feet, or half a meter). Given that information, write down the modern dimensions of the temple, according to 6:2.

3. Review 6:12–13. What does God say their covenant relationship is built on?

4. According to today's reading, on which mountain is the temple constructed? What else happened on this mountain? (See Genesis 22:2 for help.)

1. A cubit is approximately eighteen inches (one and a half feet, or half a meter). Given that information, write down the modern dimensions of Solomon's house, according to 7:2.

2. How does the author describe Hiram the craftsman in 7:14?

3. Read the description of Bezalel in Exodus 31:1–5. What do Hiram and Bezalel have in common?

4. Look up the name "Jachin" (7:21) in a Hebrew lexicon and write what you find.

5. Look up the name "Boaz" (7:21) in a Hebrew lexicon and write what you find.

6. Together, what do these two names indicate about God and His dwelling place on earth?

DAY 164 / 1 KINGS 8; 2 CHRONICLES 5

1. How does Solomon transport the ark of the covenant into the temple (8:6–8)? Given the history of moving the ark, what is significant about this?

2. Review 8:39. What unique trait does this verse acknowledge that God possesses?

3. What trait do all humans possess, according to 8:46?

4. According to 5:10, what two things are inside the ark of the covenant at this time?

5. Look up the word "glory" (5:14) in a Hebrew lexicon and write what you find.

DAY 165 / 2 CHRONICLES 6–7; PSALM 136

1. According to 6:8, what does God think of David's desire to build the temple?

2. In 6:9, how does God respond to David's desire?

3. Review 7:1. What two things does God do as a sign of His approval of the temple and the offerings?

4. Considering the context of 7:11–22, to whom is God making the promise of 7:14?

5. In Psalm 136, the psalmist praises the Lord by using three different titles. List the titles he uses in verses 2, 3, and 26.

DAY 166 / PSALMS 134, 146–150

1. Look up the word "blessed" (146:5) in a Hebrew lexicon and write what you find.

2. Review Psalm 146:7–9. It praises God for blessing nine different types of people. List the different types of people.

3. What does your list of the nine types of people God blesses reveal about God and His character?

4. How would you describe the praise represented in 149:3 and 150:3–5?

DAY 167 / 1 KINGS 9; 2 CHRONICLES 8

1. Review 9:7–8. What does God say will happen to Israel if they rebel? What does He say will happen to the temple if they rebel?

2. Based on today's reading and what we know about Solomon's wife, why doesn't Solomon want her to live in his house (8:11)?

3. Who does Solomon put to work as forced laborers?

4. Why doesn't Solomon use Israelites as slaves (see Leviticus 25:39–46 for help)?

DAY 168 / PROVERBS 25–26

1. According to 25:9–10, what should you do when you have a problem with someone else?

2. Rewrite 25:15 in your own words.

3. How would you summarize the diverse wisdom offered in 25:16–17? What one thing do these two verses have in common?

4. Review 26:4–5. How do these verses complement each other instead of contradict each other?

5. Rewrite 26:12 in your own words.

DAY 169 / **PROVERBS 27–29**

1. How would you summarize the wisdom of 27:1?

2. Rewrite 27:6 in your own words.

3. How does the wisdom of 27:6 align with the wisdom of 27:17?

4. How would you summarize the collective wisdom of 29:11 and 29:20?

5. Review 29:25. How have you seen the fear of man act as a trap in your own life?

DAY 170 / ECCLESIASTES 1–6

1. Who wrote Ecclesiastes?

2. To or for whom was it written?

3. When was it written?

4. What is the literary style (narrative, history, wisdom, prophecy, letter, etc.)?

5. Look up the word "vanity" in a Hebrew lexicon and write what you find. What is the preacher trying to indicate about the things we chase?

6. According to chapter 4, what does the preacher say drives our work ethic?

1. The message in 7:16 seems to contradict the rest of Scripture. What does the preacher seem to be pointing to in this verse? Use a study Bible for help.

2. The preacher seems to contradict himself in 7:20 and 7:29. Which of these verses holds to the rest of Scripture's teaching? What might be another possible understanding of the other verse? Use a study Bible for help.

3. What does the preacher seem to be describing in 12:1–8?

4. Rewrite 12:13 in your own words.

DAY 172 / 1 KINGS 10–11; 2 CHRONICLES 9

1. Which of God's commands in Deuteronomy 17:16–17 does Solomon break in today's reading?

2. Review God's prophetic warning in Deuteronomy 7:3–5. How do we see this coming true in today's reading?

3. What is the consequence of Solomon's rebellion? Does this seem fair to you? Why or why not?

4. Ahijah prophesies that someone will take a portion of the kingdom from Solomon. Who is it and how much will they take?

5. Who takes over Solomon's throne after he dies?

DAY 173 / PROVERBS 30–31

1. Do you see a possible prophecy of Jesus in chapter 30?

2. What four things does Agur ask God to keep him from? Why?

3. How would you summarize Lemuel's mom's advice to him in 31:8–9?

4. Rewrite 31:30 in your own words.

DAY 174 / 1 KINGS 12–14

1. How do the older advisors tell King Rehoboam to respond to the complaints of the enslaved construction workers?

2. How do King Rehoboam's friends suggest he respond to the complaints of the construction workers?

3. Whose counsel does King Rehoboam follow? What do you think his reasoning is?

4. According to 12:15, what is going on behind the scenes to impact his actions?

5. Visual search: In today's reading, Israel splits into two kingdoms. Look up a map of the divided kingdoms. Do a rough drawing here to help you remember the kingdoms. Mark the northern kingdom with its name and its first king. Mark the southern kingdom with its name and its first king.

6. What does King Jeroboam fear will happen in the northern kingdom? What does he do in response to that fear?

DAY 175 / 2 CHRONICLES 10–12

1. When Israel divides into two kingdoms, what happens to the Levites who have been dispersed across all the tribes?

2. Who or what is King Jeroboam worshipping according to 11:14–15? See Leviticus 17:7 for further insight.

3. King Rehoboam sends a new group to live among the tribes. Who are they? What is their role?

4. When does King Rehoboam abandon God's law (12:1)? What insights can we gain from this?

5. Why does God keep Egypt from destroying Jerusalem entirely?

DAY 176 / 1 KINGS 15; 2 CHRONICLES 13–16

1. Look up the phrase "high places" (1 Kings 15:14) in a Hebrew lexicon and write what you find. What is this phrase describing? Use a study Bible for help.

2. What are some of the reforms Asa makes? What one thing does he fail to do?

3. Why does King Abijah say King Jeroboam's attack will fail? Is he right or wrong?

4. At what point do you think things take a turn in Asa's reign? What do you think prompts this?

5. Review 2 Chronicles 15:3–4 and 15:5. What is the common theme in these verses? What insights can we gain from this?

DAY 177 / 1 KINGS 16; 2 CHRONICLES 17

1. Look up the word "idols" (16:13) in a Hebrew lexicon and write down what you find. What insights does this give us about idolatry?

2. All the kings in the north are evil kings. Of all the kings we read about in 1 Kings 16 today, which one is regarded as the most evil? How do you know?

3. Review 16:34. Then read Joshua 6:26. What connection do you notice between these two verses?

4. Look up the word "fear" (17:10) in a Hebrew lexicon and write down what you find. How is this different from most other references to the "fear of the LORD" that we encounter?

DAY 178 / 1 KINGS 17–19

1. In 17:1–18:20, God sends Elijah to three different locations: to the brook Cherith, to Zarephath, and to Ahab's presence. List the problems or challenges he encounters in each place.

2. How many prophets (and what types) does Elijah tell Ahab to send to meet with him at Mount Carmel?

3. How many prophets show up? Which ones are they?

4. Do a web search on Baal. What is he believed to be in charge of (i.e., "the god of")? How does this connect to the present challenge?

5. What five things are burned up in 18:38?

DAY 179 / 1 KINGS 20–21

1. When King Ben-hadad of Syria makes demands of King Ahab of Israel, Ahab agrees to most of them. With what demand does Ben-hadad cross the line?

2. Despite Ahab's wickedness, God protects him and Israel from the attacks of the Syrians twice in today's reading. What does the prophet say God is aiming to reveal in both of these scenarios?

3. After Ahab's victories, another prophet reveals how he sinned in the process. What was that sin? How does Ahab respond to the confrontation?

4. Review 21:1–3. Based on what we know about land allotments, what does Naboth mean when he says, "The LORD forbid" Ahab's request?

5. How would you describe Jezebel's actions and attitudes?

6. How does Ahab respond to God at the end of his life? What is noteworthy about this given the previous descriptions we've read of him? What does this reveal about God and His character?

DAY 180 / 1 KINGS 22; 2 CHRONICLES 18

1. Who does Jehoshaphat want to seek counsel from in 22:5? Look up that name in a Hebrew lexicon and write down what you find.

2. Who do the four hundred prophets seek counsel from in 22:6? Look up that name in a Hebrew lexicon and write down what you find.

3. Based on this distinction, we have reason to be suspicious of these four hundred prophets. Review 1 Kings 18:19–22. Given the information in questions 1 and 2 above, who are these four hundred prophets likely seeking counsel from?

4. Look up the phrase "at random" (22:34) in a Hebrew lexicon and write down what you find.

5. Review 1 Kings 18:17, 21:20, and 22:26. For most of his life, Ahab rejects the counsel of Elijah and Micaiah, but receives a prophet's counsel in 20:13. Based on this information and his words in 22:8, what is the basis of Ahab's acceptance or rejection of the words of the prophets sent to him? How can this serve as a cautionary tale for us when reading Scripture and asking God for direction?

DAY 181 / 2 CHRONICLES 19–23

1. Which group of people leads the army out to battle against the enemy coalition? Why is this an appropriate military strategy given what God has told them about the situation?

2. Judah doesn't fight in the war, but all their neighbors are afraid of them now. Why?

3. Despite God's nearness, direction, and miraculous deliverance, Judah still has a big problem according to the last half of 20:33. What is it? If they're obeying God's direction (20:32), why does this matter?

4. What sin pattern does Jehoshaphat demonstrate in today's reading (19:2, 20:37)? How does God deal with this problem in each instance?

5. Who is the unlikely protagonist of 22:10–12, and what role does she play?

1. Who wrote Obadiah?

2. To or for whom was it written?

3. When was it written?

4. What is the literary style (narrative, history, wisdom, prophecy, letter, etc.)?

5. From whom are the Edomites descended? What is their relationship to the Israelites? Do a web search if you need help.

DAY 183 / 2 KINGS 1–4

1. Look up Baal-zebub (1:2) in a Hebrew lexicon and write down what you find.

2. What does Elisha request from Elijah when he dies? How does Elijah respond to this request? What does this reveal about the nature of this request?

3. Review 1 Kings 18:38 and 2 Kings 1:10 and 1:12. How is the means of Elijah's departure fitting for the way he and God often relate?

4. When the coalition of the three kings seeks Elisha's guidance, what unique thing does he ask for before prophesying? Why do you think he makes this request?

5. Briefly summarize each of the miracles Elisha performs in chapter 4. What do these miracles point to?

DAY 184 / 2 KINGS 5–8

1. For which country is Naaman a military commander? To which country does he want to go for healing? Why is this noteworthy?

2. Why does Naaman want to take dirt from Israel back to Syria?

3. What does the king suggest they do to the Syrian captives after Elisha blinds them? What does Elisha suggest they do instead?

4. Review 6:17, 18, and 20. Who does the blinding of eyes and the opening of eyes in these passages? Why is it important to note this?

5. Judah continues to have evil kings, but God continues to spare them. According to 8:19, why is God showing them patience and mercy? What does this reveal about God and His character?

DAY 185 / 2 KINGS 9–11

1. According to 9:6–8, what two assignments does the prophet give to Jehu?

2. In what spot does Jehu assassinate King Joram of Israel and King Ahaziah of Judah? What makes this location especially fitting?

3. Review 10:11, 29, and 31. What do these three verses together reveal about Jehu and his heart?

4. What does Jehu do with the pagan temple of Baal after destroying all the worshippers?

5. What promise does God make to Jehu in 10:30?

DAY 186 / 2 KINGS 12–13; 2 CHRONICLES 24

1. Who fails to maintain the upkeep of the temple? How long does this go on? Who finally accomplishes this purpose?

2. When King Jehoahaz notices that Israel is under God's judgment, what does he do?

3. After God shows mercy to Israel, how does King Jehoahaz respond?

4. Briefly summarize and explain what happens to the man who is accidentally thrown into Elisha's grave.

5. Who warns the people and King Joash about the consequences of their sin? How does King Joash command the people to respond to this warning?

DAY 187 / 2 KINGS 14; 2 CHRONICLES 25

1. How does Amaziah defy cultural norms and honor God after taking the throne?

2. How would you summarize Jehoash's response to Amaziah in 25:18–19?

3. After Amaziah is rebuked by a man of God in 25:15, how does he respond? What does it cost him?

4. What god does Amaziah begin to worship after his victory? What is especially ironic about this?

5. Since Northern Israel repeatedly displays their wickedness, why does God only wipe out King Jeroboam's family instead of all of Northern Israel?

DAY 188 / JONAH 1–4

1. Who wrote Jonah?

2. To or for whom was it written?

3. When was it written?

4. What is the literary style (narrative, history, wisdom, prophecy, letter, etc.)?

5. Which two groups of people that Jonah encounters in this book show more regard for God and His laws than Jonah does? How do they demonstrate that?

DAY 189 / 2 KINGS 15; 2 CHRONICLES 26

1. Review 2 Kings 15:1–2 and 2 Chronicles 26:1. What other name does King Azariah go by, according to 2 Chronicles?

2. What forbidden act does Azariah want to commit? How does he respond to being rebuked?

3. What consequences does he encounter as a result of his rebellion?

4. Israel seems to be on a downward spiral, moving quickly from wicked king to wicked king. Based on 2 Kings 15:12 and 10:30, what seems to be happening here?

DAY 190 / ISAIAH 1-4

1. Who wrote Isaiah?

2. To or for whom was it written?

3. When was it written?

4. What is the literary style (narrative, history, wisdom, prophecy, letter, etc.)?

5. Which kingdom is Isaiah warning and calling to repentance? And which kingdom is he using as an example of what will happen to them if they don't repent?

6. How or why are the people's sacrifices an insult and a disgusting offering to God?

7. Do you see any prophecies of Jesus in today's reading?

DAY 191 / ISAIAH 5–8

1. Who is the vine keeper in Isaiah's poem? Who are the grapes?

2. Look up the phrase "wild grapes" in a Hebrew lexicon and write down what you find. How does this fit the context of what's happening with Israel and Judah?

3. In your Bible, circle the six "woes" of chapter 5, or note the verse references for each in your journal. In a few words, briefly describe the six types of people addressed in each woe.

4. Despite seeing the sins of others clearly, how does Isaiah personally respond when confronted with God's holiness in chapter 6?

5. What assignment does God give Isaiah in chapter 6?

6. Do you see any prophecies of Jesus in today's reading?

DAY 192 / AMOS 1–5

1. Who wrote Amos?

2. To or for whom was it written?

3. When was it written?

4. What is the literary style (narrative, history, wisdom, prophecy, letter, etc.)?

5. In your Bible, circle the eight nations God addresses in chapters 1–2, or note the verse references for each in your journal. What makes the last two unique in this list?

DAY 193 / AMOS 6–9

1. In chapter 7, what one idea do the three visions of Amos represent or foretell? What does threefold repetition typically indicate in Scripture?

2. Look up the phrase "summer fruit" (8:1) and the word "end" (8:2) in a Hebrew lexicon and write down what you find. How does this help clarify the meaning of Amos's vision?

3. What does God warn about in 8:11–12?

4. Do you see any prophecies of Jesus in today's reading?

5. What does God establish as His end goal and promise to accomplish after all the destruction and silence (9:11–15)?

DAY 194 / 2 CHRONICLES 27; ISAIAH 9–12

1. Do you see any prophecies of Jesus in today's reading?

2. It's easy for us to look at these prophecies and recognize Jesus, but how do you think the people of Isaiah's day viewed these prophecies since Jesus hadn't been born yet?

3. Why are the orphans and widows cut off in 10:1–2?

4. List the seven Spirits of 11:2. Who will be the bearer of these Spirits?

DAY 195 / MICAH 1–7

1. Who wrote Micah?

2. To or for whom was it written?

3. When was it written?

4. What is the literary style (narrative, history, wisdom, prophecy, letter, etc.)?

5. Review 2:3. Why would God destroy something He loves?

6. Review 3:5. Why does God rebuke people for declaring "peace"?

7. Do you see any prophecies of Jesus in today's reading?

DAY 196 / 2 CHRONICLES 28; 2 KINGS 16–17

1. According to 28:1–4, what kinds of sins does King Ahaz of Judah commit?

2. When God brings judgment on Judah's and Ahaz's sins via an attack from Syria and Israel, how does Ahaz respond?

3. Who does King Ahaz ask to commission an altar for him? What kind of altar is it?

4. When King Hoshea of Israel stops paying Assyria to protect them, what country do they look to for protection? How does Assyria respond?

5. When the Assyrian king wants to repopulate Samaria, who does he send to live there? What problems does this cause?

DAY 197 / ISAIAH 13–17

1. In general, who is Isaiah addressing in today's chapters? How is this approach different from what we've seen in previous chapters?

2. Briefly summarize how God will use Babylon, according to chapters 13–14.

3. Who is Isaiah referring to directly in 14:12–15?

4. Look up the phrase "Day Star" or "Star of the morning" (14:12) in a Hebrew lexicon and write down what you find. Based on this, who might Isaiah be referring to indirectly in 14:12–15? (See also Ezekiel 28:11–17.)

5. What is unique about Isaiah's oracles to Moab? How are they different from the other nations'?

DAY 198 / ISAIAH 18–22

1. How would you summarize what is prophesied in 19:16–25?

2. How does God refer to Egypt in 19:25? How does He refer to Assyria? What does this reveal about God's heart and His plan?

3. In chapter 21, Isaiah prophesies the coming destruction of Babylon. How does he mirror God's heart in this oracle?

4. Briefly summarize Isaiah's prophecy of Jerusalem in 22:1–8.

5. According to 22:9–14, how will Jerusalem respond when these events occur?

DAY 199 / ISAIAH 23–27

1. According to the focus of 23:1–12, what are the cities of Tyre and Sidon known for? What does Isaiah say God will do to these cities in the short term and the long term?

2. In chapter 24, God says the whole earth has broken a covenant with Him. What is the only covenant God has made that includes the whole earth, not just Israel specifically? See Genesis 9:8–16 for help.

3. List three passages or phrases from chapters 25–27 that were encouraging to you. What do they each reveal to you about God's character?

4. Rewrite 26:3 in your own words.

5. Review 26:12, then read John 19:28–30 and Philippians 1:6 and 2:13. What theme do these verses point to?

DAY 200 / 2 KINGS 18; 2 CHRONICLES 29–31; PSALM 48

1. According to 18:3, what unique comparison does Hezekiah receive?

2. According to 18:4, what four things does Hezekiah destroy? According to 31:1, who helps?

3. According to 30:1 and 30:17–20, what groups of people does Hezekiah invite to join in the Passover celebration? What is significant about both scenarios?

4. What do you think motivates Hezekiah's actions in 18:13–16? Is this a wise or foolish decision?

5. Why do the Assyrians wrongly think Hezekiah and the people of Judah are relying on Egypt for their strength, instead of YHWH?

DAY 201 / HOSEA 1–7

1. Who wrote Hosea?

2. To or for whom was it written?

3. When was it written?

4. What is the literary style (narrative, history, wisdom, prophecy, letter, etc.)?

5. What are the three names God has Hosea give to the children in chapter 1? How does God change these names in chapter 2?

6. According to 4:6, what has been the turning point for God's people? What has led them to fall into idolatry and turn away from God?

DAY 202 / HOSEA 8–14

1. Briefly summarize Israel's actions according to chapter 8.

2. Briefly summarize God's response to Israel's actions according to chapter 9.

3. According to 10:1–3, what has prompted Israel to forget their need for God?

4. Who will help Israel return to God (12:6)? Why is it important to note this?

5. Do you see any prophecies of Jesus in today's reading?

DAY 203 / ISAIAH 28–30

1. What particular area of overindulgence does Isaiah say the political and religious leaders both suffer from (see also Hosea 7:5)?

2. How do the leaders respond to Isaiah's rebuke (28:9–10)?

3. Do you see any prophecies of Jesus in today's reading?

4. According to 29:13 and 29:15–16, briefly describe the people in the second woe. How does God say He will respond to them (29:14, 29:17–24)? What does this reveal about His heart?

5. How would you summarize the main theme of the three woes (each chapter represents a separate woe and begins with the word "ah") in today's reading?

DAY 204 / ISAIAH 31–34

1. According to chapter 31, why shouldn't Judah rely on Egypt and their horses and chariots for strength? Where has God previously proven Himself in this area (see Exodus 14:21–31 for help)?

2. Do you see any prophecies of Jesus in today's reading?

3. How would you describe a fool, based on 32:6?

4. How would you describe a scoundrel, based on 32:7?

5. What things do the fool and the scoundrel have in common?

6. Look up the words "confusion" (or "desolation") and "emptiness" (34:11) in a Hebrew lexicon and write down what you find. Now look up Genesis 1:2 in a Hebrew lexicon and locate those words.

These verses are the only two places in Scripture where both words appear. What connection might God be pointing to in this comparison?

DAY 205 / ISAIAH 35–36

1. From your current understanding, does God's prophecy to empty and then fill the promised land seem to apply to Israel's immediate future (then) or to our future (now)? Or both?

2. What comfort(s) does God offer to fools in 35:8?

3. In chapter 36, what is the central focus of Assyria's taunts toward the people of Judah?

4. How do the people of Judah respond? Why? Does this move seem to be wise or foolish? Why?

1. When confronted with Assyria's threats, what does King Hezekiah do and where does he go immediately?

2. Assyria sends a threatening letter to King Hezekiah. After he reads it, what three steps does he take (37:14–15)?

3. When did God make His plans for what would happen with Assyria and King Sennacherib?

4. For whose sake is God saving Jerusalem (37:35)? In 38:5, how does God identify Himself? What might be significant or connected about these two references?

5. How does the foolish decision Hezekiah makes near the end of his life echo the foolish decision he made earlier in his reign (2 Kings 18:13–16)? Are there any themes or ideas connecting these two instances?

DAY 207 / ISAIAH 40–43

1. Instead of YHWH, who does Israel look to for help, according to 40:26?

2. Isaiah prophesies that even after Israel is restored to their land, they will still have issues. What belief about God seems to be the root of their problem, according to 40:27?

3. Look up the word "wait" (40:31) in a Hebrew lexicon and write down what you find. How does this impact your understanding of this verse?

4. What theme does God repeat to His people in chapter 41? Why?

5. Do you see any prophecies of Jesus in today's reading?

1. If Cyrus is a pagan king (45:4–5), how can he be referred to as God's "shepherd" (44:28) and His "anointed" one (45:1)?

2. In chapter 46, Isaiah paints a picture of Babylon having to carry something around. What is it? He also says God is carrying something around. What is it? How do these two images stand in contrast to each other?

3. When God brings judgment on Babylon for the way they treated Israel, who will they turn to for help? Will that serve them well?

4. How would you summarize the problem Isaiah attributes to Israel when he addresses them in 48:1?

5. According to 48:9–11, why does God withhold His anger toward Israel? Is this a fitting reason? Why or why not?

1. Review 19:7. Who is the active agent (i.e., the liar) in misleading Sennacherib?

2. What does 19:7 reveal about God? (If you struggle with this passage, look up Hebrews 6:18, John 14:6, and Romans 8:28 to see a fuller picture of what's happening here.)

3. In Assyria's war against Judah, how many are fighting on Assyria's side? How many are fighting on Judah's side?

4. Who is the psalmist referring to in 46:5? How did you see this truth confirmed in 2 Kings 19?

5. Who is the psalmist referring to in the poetic language of 80:7? What is 80:9 referring to?

DAY 210 / ISAIAH 49–53

1. Israel is waiting for God's promises to them to be fulfilled, and God tells them they won't be put to shame (49:23). Why or how can waiting sometimes feel shameful?

2. Do you see any prophecies of Jesus in chapter 50?

3. Chapters 52–53 are filled with some of the richest, clearest Old Testament prophecies of Jesus. What does 53:2 reveal about His appearance?

4. According to 52:14, how severe was the beating Jesus endured prior to and during His crucifixion?

5. Did you discover anything new about Jesus while reading chapters 52–53?

DAY 211 / ISAIAH 54–58

1. God repeatedly compares His relationship with Israel to a marriage (see 54:5). They've been unfaithful, but He keeps pursuing them. They'll go into exile, but He'll bring them back (like Hosea did with Gomer). Given that context, what do you think He's communicating to Israel in 54:1–3?

2. What is God offering people in 55:1–2? Does this appear to be literal or figurative? How much will it cost them?

3. What kind of covenant does God mention in 55:3? How will this covenant be different from the covenant He made with Israel previously?

4. How would you describe Israel's leaders based on 56:9–12?

5. Based on chapter 58, how would you summarize the wrong kind of fasting? How would you summarize the right kind of fasting?

6. What's your primary takeaway from these two examples in chapter 58?

DAY 212 / ISAIAH 59–63

1. The confession in 59:10–15 is part of what is likely Israel's confession of their sins and the consequences that follow. How would you summarize their thoughts and feelings?

2. According to 59:16–20, who comes to their rescue?

3. If the "them" (plural) of 59:21 refers to Israel, who does the "you" (Hebrew singular) refer to? Does this change the way you understand the verse? Why or why not?

4. Do you see any prophecies of Jesus in chapter 60?

5. Do you see any prophecies of Jesus in chapter 61?

6. Isaiah 61–62 describes the year of the Lord's favor, and Isaiah 63 describes the day of His wrath. These timelines may be poetic images and metaphors, but they represent a greater reality. If we imagine these to be fixed timelines, how much more favor is God showing than wrath?

DAY 213 / ISAIAH 64–66

1. Look up the word "polluted" (64:6), or "filthy," in a Hebrew lexicon and write down what you find. What is Isaiah saying about their attempts at righteous deeds?

2. As you think back through our recent reading, what types of "righteous deeds" or religious actions have these people been doing?

3. Review 65:17–25. Why do we need God to create a new earth? (See Genesis 3 for help.) Why do we need God to create a new heaven? (See Revelation 12:7–12 for help.)

4. According to 66:16 and 66:20, who will God gather to see His glory?

5. According to 66:21, what role will He give some of those Gentile outsiders? Why is this noteworthy?

DAY 214 / 2 KINGS 20–21

1. Review 20:1 and 20:5–6. Why is there a difference between what God says and what He does? Did He lie or change His mind, or is there another possible option that helps explain this?

2. What major work of Hezekiah does his son Manasseh undo immediately after his death?

3. Of all the terrible things Manasseh does during his reign, which is most troubling to you? Why?

4. According to 21:9, 11, and 16, who else is impacted by Manasseh's sins? What lesson can we learn from this?

DAY 215 / 2 CHRONICLES 32–33

1. Review 32:7–8. What challenge does Hezekiah offer his army? What encouragement does he give toward that end?

2. Review 32:23. Who is exalted? What role might this play in what happens in the rest of Hezekiah's life?

3. Review 33:10–13. Divide this passage into five phases. Give a name to each phase.

4. Based on question 3, what is the turning point in Manasseh's story?

DAY 216 / NAHUM 1–3

1. Who wrote Nahum?

2. To or for whom was it written?

3. When was it written?

4. What is the literary style (narrative, history, wisdom, prophecy, letter, etc.)?

5. Compare 1:2–3 to Exodus 34:6–7. Who is being addressed in each passage? How are the two passages similar? What's different about them?

DAY 217 / 2 KINGS 22–23; 2 CHRONICLES 34–35

1. Briefly summarize King Josiah's response to Hilkiah's discovery.

2. In 2 Kings 20:16–19, King Hezekiah received news similar to what King Josiah receives today in 22:18–23:3. How do their responses vary?

3. Look up the word "necromancers" (23:24) and write down what you find.

4. What do you think motivates Josiah's actions toward Pharaoh Neco in the battle against the Babylonians? Does this change your view of him? Why or why not?

5. After Josiah's son Jehoahaz dies, who appoints Judah's next king? What is significant about this?

DAY 218 / ZEPHANIAH 1–3

1. Who wrote Zephaniah?

2. To or for whom was it written?

3. When was it written?

4. What is the literary style (narrative, history, wisdom, prophecy, letter, etc.)?

5. Do you see any prophecies of Jesus in today's reading?

6. Rewrite 3:15 in your own words.

DAY 219 / JEREMIAH 1–3

1. Who wrote Jeremiah?

2. To or for whom was it written?

3. When was it written?

4. What is the literary style (narrative, history, wisdom, prophecy, letter, etc.)?

5. What three things does God promise in 1:19?

DAY 220 / JEREMIAH 4–6

1. Summarize the significance of 4:4 in your own words.

2. In 4:10, Jeremiah accuses God of lying to him. Is he right or wrong in this accusation? Why?

3. What picture is Jeremiah painting in 4:23–26, and what does this indicate about God's plans for His creation? (Review Genesis 1:2 for help.)

4. Review 6:13–15. For each verse, briefly summarize or name the type of sin being committed in Jeremiah's prophecy.

DAY 221 / JEREMIAH 7–9

1. According to Jeremiah's warning in 7:4, what do the people seem to be putting their trust in? What's wrong with that?

2. What warning does God give to Jeremiah directly about his own actions? Why?

3. According to 8:18–9:6, what two primary feelings does Jeremiah have toward the people of Judah? Which feeling do you connect with most? Why?

4. Rewrite 9:23–24 in your own words.

5. Ultimately, why is circumcision of the flesh insufficient, according to 9:25–26?

DAY 222 / JEREMIAH 10–13

1. Summarize the two descriptions of poor leaders and the two results of poor leadership in 10:21.

2. What things are the people looking to their idols to provide for them?

3. In modern society, we're less likely to set up actual idols to give us what you listed in response to question 2, but we're not immune to idolatry. What possessions or practices do we look to today in order to gain those kinds of things?

4. According to 11:18–20, what's happening in Jeremiah's personal life as a result of his prophecies?

5. Summarize the promise God makes in 12:16. To whom is it made?

DAY 223 / JEREMIAH 14–17

1. Trace the conversation in chapter 14. Who is likely praying the prayer in verses 7–9?

2. What punishments does God promise the people?

3. The list from question 2 contains the exact things the false prophets say won't happen. Based on 14:13–15, do you think the prophets are intentionally deceiving the people, or are they also misled? Why?

4. According to chapter 15, what is the fourth possible option for punishment not previously listed?

5. What command does God give Jeremiah in 16:1–2? Does this contradict God's words in Genesis 1:28 and 9:7? Why or why not?

DAY 224 / JEREMIAH 18–22

1. What lesson does Jeremiah learn during his visit to the potter's house?

2. Today, Jeremiah's patience with the people ends and he begins to pray not for them, but against them. What causes him to reach this point?

3. According to chapter 21, what is the only hope for survival for the people of Jerusalem?

4. Briefly summarize the two messages Jeremiah sends to King Zedekiah in chapters 21 and 22.

5. Look up the word "Chaldeans" (22:25) in a Hebrew lexicon (*Gesenius' Hebrew-Chaldee Lexicon* is especially helpful). Who are the Chaldeans?

DAY 225 / JEREMIAH 23–25

1. Do you see any prophecies of Jesus in today's reading?

2. Why are the sins of Judah (and its capital, Jerusalem) worse than the sins of Israel (and its capital, Samaria)? What lesson can we learn from this?

3. According to chapter 25, how long will the people of Judah be in exile? Where will they be in exile? What will happen to their captors afterward?

4. What do the good figs represent? What will happen to them?

5. What do the bad figs represent? What will happen to them?

DAY 226 / JEREMIAH 26–29

1. Review Jeremiah's prophecy in 26:2–6, then compare it to the religious leaders' accusation of him in 26:9. What part do they leave out when recounting his words?

2. Only one group of people is even willing to consider Jeremiah's prophecies and take them seriously. Who are they? Why do you think they're willing to listen?

3. What message is God conveying through the yoke He calls Jeremiah to wear?

4. How does God refer to Nebuchadnezzar, king of Babylon, in 27:6? What does it mean that God uses this description here?

5. Why do you think there's so much resistance against Jeremiah's prophecies among the priests, leaders, and other prophets?

1. In your Bible, underline all the things God says He will do for Judah and Israel in chapter 30 (or list them out).

2. Who has Judah been focused on serving while they've been sinning and rebelling? Who are they serving in 30:8? Who are they serving in 30:9?

3. Do you see any prophecies of Jesus in today's reading?

4. Since God's plan for the Messiah is connected specifically to the tribe of Judah, why does He include all the other tribes of Israel in His plan to prosper them (31:1), especially given that the kingdom of Northern Israel has been so wicked?

5. We've already seen God's promise of the everlasting covenant in Isaiah 55:3, and today we see Jeremiah prophesying the same thing. What verses in today's reading point to this?

1. What is the significance of Jeremiah's buying the plot of land in chapter 32? Why is this important on a spiritual level?

2. What challenges and doubts does Jeremiah express after going through with the purchase? How does he handle them?

3. What three things does God say He will do for Israel in 32:40? What do each of these reveal about Him and His attributes?

4. What covenant does King Zedekiah break with the people? What consequences does God give him?

5. Do you see any prophecies of Jesus in today's reading?

1. Yesterday's reading ended with a story of Judah's unfaithfulness; today's opens with a story of the Rechabites' extreme faithfulness. Why do you think Scripture puts these two stories back to back?

2. Even though they aren't Israelites, what blessing does God extend to the Rechabites? What does this reveal about God and His character?

3. How do the officials respond to Baruch's reading of Jeremiah's scroll? How does the king respond?

4. What misunderstanding leads to Jeremiah's arrest?

5. How does God use Jeremiah's imprisonment to bless him and to advance his message?

DAY 230 / JEREMIAH 38–40; PSALMS 74, 79

1. Why do the officials want to put Jeremiah in prison?

2. Describe Jeremiah's relationship with King Zedekiah in today's reading.

3. According to 39:1–2, how much time passes during which Zedekiah could recall and obey God's commands? What does this reveal about God?

4. Review 38:12–13 and 39:15–18. Then read Joshua 2:15 and 6:15–17. How many parallels do you see in these two stories?

DAY 231 / 2 KINGS 24–25; 2 CHRONICLES 36

1. Josiah is the last good king of Judah, then there are four more kings. Give a brief description of the final four kings of Judah.

2. Based on what you know so far, how would you describe the relationship between a vassal nation and its lord?

3. Which king is taken into captivity in Egypt? Which king is taken into captivity in Babylon?

4. Which king surrenders to Babylon? Why is this noteworthy, based on Jeremiah's prophecies?

5. Based on what we know about Cyrus, king of Persia, what's so remarkable about 36:22–23?

DAY 232 / HABAKKUK 1–3

1. Who wrote Habakkuk?

2. To or for whom was it written?

3. When was it written?

4. What is the literary style (narrative, history, wisdom, prophecy, letter, etc.)?

5. Why does Habakkuk initially think God isn't listening to him? Is he right or wrong? Why?

DAY 233 / JEREMIAH 41–45

1. What does God tell the people of Judah to do in order to survive? Why does this seem counterintuitive?

2. What do they do instead?

3. Describe the sign-act God commands in 43:9–11. What is God describing to Jeremiah?

4. According to Jeremiah 44:7, who is responsible for this consequence—Judah? Babylon? God? And why?

5. Why do the people of Judah think they've been carried off into captivity?

1. Who is God sending to attack Egypt? What will happen to the Israelites who are in Egypt when the enemy attacks? What does this reveal about God's character?

2. What (metaphorical) tool is God using when He confronts the Philistines for their sins against Him and His people?

3. According to 48:7, what two things has Moab relied on? According to 48:26 and 42, what sin has Moab committed? How are these two ideas connected?

4. In general, how would you describe Moab based on what you read in chapter 48?

5. What promise does God make to Moab at the end of the oracle? What does this reveal about His character?

DAY 235 / JEREMIAH 49–50

1. Why do you think God promises to show mercy to the Ammonites?

2. Based on what you know, who are the Edomites descended from? What is their relationship to the Israelites?

3. Who does God promise to care for in Edom?

4. What other place(s) or people(s) does God promise to show kindness to? Why?

5. Look up the word "pardon" (50:20) in a Hebrew lexicon and write down what you find. Based on that, why will there be no iniquity or sin among God's people?

DAY 236 / JEREMIAH 51–52

1. In today's reading, Jeremiah prophesies the downfall of Babylon, which is where the exiles of Judah are living. What does God say to Babylon about His people in 51:5?

2. Review 51:11, 24, 35–37, and 49. What is God promising Babylon? And why?

3. Review 51:6, 45–46, and 50. What are God's instructions (practical and spiritual) to His people during this time?

4. Review 51:26 and 54–56. Compare and contrast the Israelites' departure from Babylonian captivity with their exodus from Egyptian slavery.

5. In chapter 52, Jeremiah recounts the fulfillment of some tragic prophecies but ends the whole book with four verses in a different tone. Why do you think he chooses to end with this particular story?

DAY 237 / LAMENTATIONS 1–2

1. Who wrote Lamentations?

2. To or for whom was it written?

3. When was it written?

4. What is the literary style (narrative, history, wisdom, prophecy, letter, etc.)?

5. What do the people of Judah spend their time remembering?

6. Do you see any signs of true repentance in Judah's response to what happened? Do they believe God's actions are justified?

DAY 238 / LAMENTATIONS 3–5

1. Review 3:25–27. How would you summarize this passage and its ideas in your own words?

2. Did God cause or allow these things to happen to Jerusalem? Is the distinction important? Why or why not?

3. Look up the word "willingly" (3:33 NIV) and write down what you find. What does this reveal about God's motives behind bringing affliction?

4. Do God's motives matter in the question of His level of involvement in Jerusalem's destruction? Why or why not?

5. While the author credits God for Jerusalem's destruction, he ends with a chapter-long prayer praising God and asking Him to restore them to Himself. What does this indicate about the author's understanding of God and His actions?

DAY 239 / EZEKIEL 1–4

1. Who wrote Ezekiel?

2. To or for whom was it written?

3. When was it written?

4. What is the literary style (narrative, history, wisdom, prophecy, letter, etc.)?

5. Read Psalm 18:10 and Ezekiel 10:3–22. Compare these descriptions with Ezekiel's vision in chapter 1. What is he likely seeing in chapter 1?

6. How long does God call Ezekiel to lie on his side? Based on what you know about prophets, why would God ask him to do this?

DAY 240 / EZEKIEL 5–8

1. In your Bible, underline every use of the phrase "they shall know that I am the LORD" in today's reading, or make a note of the references here.

2. God tells Ezekiel to perform sign-acts pointing to the types of destruction He will bring, but God actually promised these consequences long ago (see Leviticus 20:14, 21:9, and 26:21–39). Why do you think the Israelites failed to believe God's warning?

3. Based on 7:19, what is the root of the sins of the people?

4. How does the remnant get selected to be the remnant?

5. Is the remnant repentant of their sins?

1. In your Bible, underline every use of the phrase "they shall know that I am the LORD" in today's reading, or make a note of the references here.

2. God summons seven executioners and assigns them two different roles. What role does He assign to the one dressed in linen? What role does He assign to the other six?

3. Look up the word "mark" (9:4) in a Hebrew lexicon and write down what you find about its meaning. Also, write the Hebrew transliteration (i.e., the word spelled out using English letters).

4. "Tav" is the last letter of the Hebrew alphabet. Do a web search for "early Hebrew letter tav," and draw the letter below. What do you notice about it?

5. After the executioners have done their jobs, where does God tell them to put the bodies? What's peculiar about this command?

6. Look up the phrase used for the word "stood" (10:19) in a Hebrew lexicon and write down what you find. It will consist of one word repeated. What's noteworthy about the repetition here?

7. When God leaves the temple, where does He go? What's noteworthy about this?

DAY 242 / EZEKIEL 13–15

1. In your Bible, underline every use of the phrase "they shall know that I am the LORD" in today's reading, or make a note of the references here.

2. How would you summarize God's warning to the false prophets in 13:9–16? Is this warning metaphorical or literal? If metaphorical, what does it represent?

3. What two specific categories of lies does God speak against in 13:22? If God hates these lies, what does this tell us about what God desires and loves?

4. Does God agree to speak with the rebellious elders in chapter 14? Summarize His words to them.

5. Based on what you know or remember, what things do the men listed in 14:20 have in common?

DAY 243 / EZEKIEL 16–17

1. In your Bible, underline every use of the phrase "they shall know that I am the LORD" in today's reading, or make a note of the references here.

2. In your Bible, underline the nineteen verbs used to describe God's actions toward Israel in chapter 16, or list them here.

3. What things does the woman put her trust in? What thing(s) might this metaphor represent for the Israelites?

4. According to 16:49–50, list the sins of Sodom. List their sins of thought and attitude first, then list their sins of action and inaction.

5. Do you see any prophecies of Jesus in today's reading?

DAY 244 / EZEKIEL 18–20

1. In your Bible, underline every use of the phrase "they shall know that I am the LORD" in today's reading, or make a note of the references here.

2. In 18:1–18, what do the people seem to misunderstand? What point does God make in correcting them?

3. According to 18:19 and 25, what do they think of God's explanation?

4. Review 18:23 and 32. What do these verses reveal about God and His character?

5. In chapter 20, how many times does God relent from bringing disaster despite the people's persistent rebellion?

6. Given the context, what do you think God is communicating in 20:25–26?

DAY 245 / EZEKIEL 21–22

1. In your Bible, underline every use of the phrase "they shall know that I am the LORD" in today's reading, or make a note of the references here.

2. According to 21:4, what two types of people will God cut off?

3. In 21:18–23, what decision is King Nebuchadnezzar of Babylon trying to make? What is the result?

4. Look up the word "dross" (22:18) in a Hebrew lexicon and write down what you find. (*Gesenius' Hebrew-Chaldee Lexicon* is especially helpful.) What is God communicating about Israel through this comparison? Based on what you know, does this seem like an accurate comparison?

5. How many righteous men does God find among them, according to 22:30? How does this help inform your understanding of 21:4?

DAY 246 / EZEKIEL 23–24

1. In your Bible, underline every use of the phrase "they shall know that I am the LORD" in today's reading, or make a note of the references here.

2. What two cities do the two women represent in chapter 23? Why is God addressing these two cities specifically? What is the general message He sends them?

3. Trace the thread of sin in 23:7. What is Samaria's first sin? What sin does it lead to?

4. How would you summarize the metaphor in 24:6–13? What is God saying about Jerusalem and its people?

5. What unusual command does God give Ezekiel regarding his wife's death? Given Ezekiel's role, what purpose might God be trying to accomplish?

DAY 247 / EZEKIEL 25–27

1. In your Bible, underline every use of the phrase "they shall know that I am the LORD" in today's reading, or make a note of the references here.

2. How would you summarize God's main indictment against the Ammonites?

3. How would you summarize God's main indictment against the Moabites?

4. Who will God send to seek retribution against the Edomites?

5. What is Tyre known for? How does God seem to feel about Tyre based on chapter 27?

DAY 248 / EZEKIEL 28–30

1. In your Bible, underline every use of the phrase "they shall know that I am the LORD" in today's reading, or make a note of the references here.

2. What claim does the leader of Tyre make about himself? How does YHWH respond to this claim?

3. In 28:11–19, who is God addressing? Who is God describing? How do these two individuals correspond to each other?

4. Based on 29:3, how would you summarize Egypt's attitude? Who will eventually come to destroy Egypt?

DAY 249 / EZEKIEL 31–33

1. In your Bible, underline every use of the phrase "they shall know that I am the LORD" in today's reading, or make a note of the references here.

2. Who is God talking to in chapter 31? Who is God talking about? How would you summarize what God is communicating in this chapter?

3. Why don't the other nations celebrate the downfall of mighty Egypt?

4. Look up the word "watchman" (33:7) in a Hebrew lexicon and write down what you find. How do this word and its definition help explain Ezekiel's role?

5. Review 33:10–20. What does God want the people to know about how to have a relationship with Him?

DAY 250 / EZEKIEL 34–36

1. In your Bible, underline every use of the phrase "they shall know that I am the LORD" in today's reading, or make a note of the references here.

2. Why is God committed to giving Israel the land?

3. Review 36:22–38. In your Bible, underline all the verbs God uses to describe what He will do in His plan for restoration, or list them here.

4. What is the only past tense verb in this list? Why is this important to note?

5. What does God's plan for restoration and His involvement in that plan reveal about His character?

DAY 251 / EZEKIEL 37–39

1. In your Bible, underline every use of the phrase "they shall know that I am the LORD" in today's reading, or make a note of the references here.

2. In Ezekiel's vision, who commands the bones to live? By what process does this happen?

3. What or who do the bones represent in this vision? What is God communicating to Ezekiel in this vision?

4. What or who do the sticks represent in Ezekiel's sign-act? What is God communicating through this sign-act?

5. Why does God say He will bring Gog against His people and land? What will happen when Gog comes to attack?

6. Do you see any prophecies of Jesus in today's reading?

DAY 252 / EZEKIEL 40–42

1. Where are the people of Israel when God gives Ezekiel this temple vision?

2. What day is the fourteenth day of the first month?

3. What might God's motive be for discussing the temple in this place and at this time?

4. According to 40:35–38, by what gate are the sacrifices made? See Leviticus 1:11 for help.

5. How high (in feet or meters) is the outer wall, according to 40:5? What is the purpose of this wall, according to 42:20? What do the height and the purpose indicate about the nature of this wall?

DAY 253 / EZEKIEL 43–45

1. According to 43:1–5, which gate does God use when He enters Israel? What will happen to this gate, according to 44:1–2?

2. What impact are the dimensions of the temple intended to have on the people when they hear them?

3. In chapter 44, God meets with Ezekiel on Mount Moriah to issue new laws, just like He met with Moses on Mount Sinai to issue laws. How are these new laws different?

4. Why would God change or add to the laws He has revealed to His people up to this point?

5. What specific things does God call the princes of Israel to focus on first and foremost? How does this speak to what they've been through in the past?

DAY 254 / EZEKIEL 46–48

1. In 46:16–18, what does God forbid the political leaders from doing? How does this speak to the problems they've previously had?

2. What adjustment does God make for the Levites in 48:11–14? What does this reveal about God?

3. Review 48:30–34. Do the math to convert cubits to modern measurements (feet or meters). According to your math, what are the dimensions of the city gates?

DAY 255 / JOEL 1–3

1. Who wrote Joel?

2. To or for whom was it written?

3. When was it written?

4. What is the literary style (narrative, history, wisdom, prophecy, letter, etc.)?

5. How would you summarize what God is communicating in 2:12–14?

6. What does it mean that God "became jealous for his land" in 2:18?

DAY 256 / DANIEL 1–3

1. Who wrote Daniel?

2. To or for whom was it written?

3. When was it written?

4. What is the literary style (narrative, history, wisdom, prophecy, letter, etc.)?

5. What theme do you notice about God in 1:9, 1:17, and 2:37–38?

6. Review Daniel 2:20–23 and list all the things Daniel says God is sovereign over.

DAY 257 / DANIEL 4–6

1. How does Daniel say King Nebuchadnezzar can delay his punishment? Does the king comply?

2. In what three different ways does God speak to King Nebuchadnezzar in chapter 4?

3. Why do you think the interpreters can't read the writing on the wall?

4. How would you summarize Daniel's rebuke of King Belshazzar?

5. Who begins ruling in Babylon after King Belshazzar's death? How does the new ruler feel about Daniel?

DAY 258 / DANIEL 7–9

1. Why can't Daniel interpret his dream in chapter 7? Who helps him? What does this reveal about Daniel?

2. Based on what you know so far, what two things (one is a trait and the other is an entity) does the image of a horn often represent in Scripture?

3. Based on what you know so far, what does the number seven often symbolize in Scripture? Based on that, what would the number three and a half likely symbolize?

4. Who is the Son of Man? See Mark 14:61–62 for help.

5. Why is Daniel grieved to find out that the seventy years of captivity are almost over?

6. Look up the phrase "swift flight" (9:21) in a Hebrew lexicon and write down what you find. Who is this phrase likely referring to? How does that impact your understanding of the situation?

DAY 259 / DANIEL 10–12

1. With whom has the angel been fighting? Based on your current understanding, is this a person, a spiritual power, some combination of the two, etc.?

2. When Daniel hears information about what's happening in the spiritual realm, he struggles with it. How does God bring comfort to him?

3. What is the name of the angel who helps in the fight? What else is this angel assigned to, according to 12:1?

4. What does chapter 11 reveal about the means and limits of earthly powers?

5. How does God respond to Daniel's question in 12:8?

DAY 260 / EZRA 1–3

1. Who wrote Ezra?

2. To or for whom was it written?

3. When was it written?

4. What is the literary style (narrative, history, wisdom, prophecy, letter, etc.)?

5. According to 1:1–3, what charge does God give to King Cyrus of Persia? What's noteworthy about this scenario?

6. Look up the phrase "freewill offering" (3:5) and write down what you find.

7. Why can't the older generation celebrate the rebuilding of the temple?

DAY 261 / EZRA 4–6; PSALM 137

1. Why don't Zerubbabel and Joshua let the locals help rebuild the temple?

2. What do the locals do each time a new king (Ahasuerus and Artaxerxes) takes the throne?

3. In chapter 5, what prompts the Jews to start rebuilding again?

4. What surprising news is discovered when the political leaders search the archives for the building permit for the temple?

DAY 262 / HAGGAI 1–2

1. Who wrote Haggai?

2. To or for whom was it written?

3. When was it written?

4. What is the literary style (narrative, history, wisdom, prophecy, letter, etc.)?

5. What particular sin does Haggai confront the people about?

6. If the holiness of God's presence can be transmitted via the priests' garments (Ezekiel 44:19), why can't the holiness of meat be transferred to other foods?

7. What point of comparison is Haggai trying to make with the questions he's asking Jeshua the high priest?

DAY 263 / ZECHARIAH 1–4

1. Who wrote Zechariah?

2. To or for whom was it written?

3. When was it written?

4. What is the literary style (narrative, history, wisdom, prophecy, letter, etc.)?

5. According to 1:6, what significant thing happened during the exile? Why is this significant?

6. In Zechariah's visions, what is God's general message to the nations who have opposed Israel?

DAY 264 / ZECHARIAH 5–9

1. Which two laws are mentioned in the vision of the flying scroll? Why do you think only these two laws are mentioned?

2. In the vision of the flying basket, where does "Wickedness" land and make its home? (If you're unfamiliar with the location, do a web search to find out what area is being referenced.) What does this vision symbolize?

3. Both visions one and eight feature horses. What do horses often represent in Scripture (see Psalm 20:7 for help)? Why do you think they feature prominently in Zechariah's night of visions?

4. Do you see any prophecies of Jesus in today's reading? What stands out to you most in these prophecies?

DAY 265 / ZECHARIAH 10–14

1. In chapter 10, God makes a lot of promises to Israel. What literal implications does this have for them? What spiritual implications does it have for us today?

2. In chapter 11, Zechariah is called to shepherd a flock. Do you think this flock is literal (a sign-act) or a prophetic parable? Why?

3. How does he initially respond to the flock? What changes and why?

4. What payout does he get for his services, and what does God tell him to do with it?

5. Do you see any prophecies of Jesus in today's reading?

DAY 266 / ESTHER 1–5

1. Who wrote Esther?

2. To or for whom was it written?

3. When was it written?

4. What is the literary style (narrative, history, wisdom, prophecy, letter, etc.)?

5. On what day are the letters announcing the slaughter of the Jews sent throughout the provinces? Why is this significant?

DAY 267 / ESTHER 6–10

1. Since the king is unable to reverse his edict, what loophole does he suggest?

2. Does the new edict keep the Persians from attacking the Jews?

3. What aspect of the new edict do the Jews not take advantage of? Why do you think they respond that way?

4. According to 9:26–32, what new law do the Jews put in place as a result of these events?

DAY 268 / EZRA 7–10

1. What do you think it means that Ezra was "skilled in the Law of Moses" (7:6)? How do verses 10 and 11 help us understand that phrase better?

2. When King Artaxerxes sends Jews back to Jerusalem from Persia, what does he send with them? What financial promise does he make them?

3. Who does Ezra credit for the king's kindness and generosity? Why is this noteworthy?

4. What does Ezra do when he grows fearful during the journey back to Jerusalem from Persia?

5. Why does Ezra forbid marrying non-Jews (Canaanites, etc.)? Is this a new idea?

DAY 269 / NEHEMIAH 1–5

1. Who wrote Nehemiah?

2. To or for whom was it written?

3. When was it written?

4. What is the literary style (narrative, history, wisdom, prophecy, letter, etc.)?

5. What alarming news does Nehemiah receive about what's happening back in Jerusalem?

6. What are the three pieces of instruction Nehemiah gives to his construction crew in 4:14? How do these three pieces work together harmoniously?

DAY 270 / NEHEMIAH 6–7

1. What lies are fabricated about Nehemiah and the Jews in the fifth letter from his enemies?

2. What piece of advice from Shemaiah makes Nehemiah suspicious of him? Why?

3. Even with all the opposition, how long does the rebuilding project take? Why do the other nations take note of this?

4. What traits does Nehemiah look for when hiring someone for the role of castle governor? Why are these traits important for this role?

DAY 271 / NEHEMIAH 8–10

1. What different physical positions do the people take while listening to Ezra and Nehemiah read the Word of God?

2. Who helps the people understand what Ezra and Nehemiah are reading to them?

3. What celebration do the people realize they've forgotten? What does it commemorate?

4. How would you describe the prayer in 9:6–38?

5. What is the one request this prayer makes of God?

6. At this point in the story, are you hopeful for the people of Jerusalem? Why or why not?

DAY 272 / NEHEMIAH 11–13; PSALM 126

1. How do the people of Jerusalem determine who will live inside the city gates versus outside them?

2. What do they discover while reading the Book of Moses? How do they respond to this discovery?

3. How would you describe Nehemiah's response to Tobiah's actions in chapter 13? Do you think his anger is justified and righteous? Why or why not?

4. What three major signs in chapter 13 indicate that the people of Jerusalem are collectively taking a turn for the worse and returning to their old sin patterns?

5. Which of these three things makes Nehemiah the angriest? Why do you think it provokes the strongest response from him?

DAY 273 / MALACHI 1–4

1. Who wrote Malachi?

2. To or for whom was it written?

3. When was it written?

4. What is the literary style (narrative, history, wisdom, prophecy, letter, etc.)?

5. What piece of advice does Malachi give twice in 2:15–16? How would you summarize this advice? Why is it so important that he repeats it?

6. Summarize the two accusations the people of Judah make against God in 2:17. Are these accusations right or wrong? Explain.

7. There are two messengers referenced in 3:1. Based on what you know so far, who are they? (See Matthew 11:7–11, Mark 1:1–8, and John 1:6–8 for help.)

DAY 274 / LUKE 1; JOHN 1

1. Who wrote Luke?

2. To or for whom was it written?

3. When was it written?

4. What is the literary style (narrative, history, wisdom, prophecy, letter, etc.)?

5. Who is the first human to prophesy aloud that Mary is pregnant with the Messiah? What's noteworthy about this?

6. When Zechariah can finally speak again, what does he praise God for?

7. Who wrote John?

8. To or for whom was it written?

9. When was it written?

10. What is the literary style (narrative, history, wisdom, prophecy, letter, etc.)?

11. Who specifically does John credit with doing the manual labor of creation?

12. What supernatural ability does Jesus possess that convinces Nathanael to follow Him?

DAY 275 / MATTHEW 1; LUKE 2

1. Who wrote Matthew?

2. To or for whom was it written?

3. When was it written?

4. What is the literary style (narrative, history, wisdom, prophecy, letter, etc.)?

5. Does anything stand out to you as unique about Matthew's genealogy?

6. Does Mary remain a virgin after the birth of Jesus (1:18, 25)?

7. What offering do Mary and Joseph bring to the temple when they go to present Jesus there? What does this reveal about them? (See Leviticus 12:8 for help.)

DAY 276 / MATTHEW 2

1. Where is Jesus when the wise men come to visit Him?

2. How would you describe King Herod based on today's reading?

3. Based on contextual clues, roughly how old is Jesus when the wise men come to visit Him?

4. What does it reveal about God that He would draw the wise men from the east to come worship Jesus?

DAY 277 / MATTHEW 3; MARK 1; LUKE 3

1. Who wrote Mark?

2. To or for whom was it written?

3. When was it written?

4. What is the literary style (narrative, history, wisdom, prophecy, letter, etc.)?

5. Why does John the Baptist refuse to baptize the Pharisees and Sadducees? What does this reveal to us about baptism?

6. What distinct roles do the three persons of the Trinity (Father, Son, Spirit) serve in the story of Jesus's baptism?

7. During the disciples' first few days of following Jesus, what are the things they see Him display His power over?

DAY 278 / MATTHEW 4; LUKE 4–5

1. Look up the word "devil" (Matthew 4:1) in a Greek lexicon and write down what you find. What part of speech is the Greek word used here? What does it mean?

2. What tool does the devil use to try to trick and entice Jesus? How does Jesus fight back? What noteworthy thing does this encounter reveal?

3. Rewrite Jesus's message in Matthew 4:17 in your own words.

4. According to Luke 4:1 and 4:14, by what power and leading does Jesus go into the wilderness and return from the wilderness? Why is this important to note?

5. How do the people in the synagogue first respond to Jesus when He reveals that He is the fulfillment of the Scriptures? What does He say that makes them respond differently?

1. Why do you think Jesus initially resists his mother's request? What does he mean by "my hour has not yet come" (2:4)?

2. As John jumps ahead in the timeline to the last week of Jesus's life, we see a very different scene—one where Jesus is demonstrative in His actions, not reserved like He was with the water-to-wine miracle. In this instance, He makes a whip and turns over the tables in the temple. What do you think accounts for the change in His approach?

3. To what does Jesus compare His body? What connection(s) do you see between the way the people treat Him and the way they treat the thing He compares it to?

4. In Jesus's talk with Nicodemus, what things does He share about the work of the Holy Spirit? What roles does the Spirit serve in the lives of believers?

5. According to 3:36, who does Jesus say is under God's wrath? Who is not under God's wrath?

6. Why do the Jews avoid Samaritans? Use a study Bible for help.

DAY 280 / MATTHEW 8; MARK 2

1. How would you describe the leper's request? What tones and attitudes does it convey?

2. Why do you think Jesus told the leper to keep quiet about the miracle, like He also did in Luke 5:12–14, but the woman at the well in John 4 was allowed to tell everyone?

3. Who approaches Jesus in Capernaum to ask for His help? What's noteworthy about the fact that this person asks for His help?

4. How would you summarize Jesus's message in Matthew 8:10–12?

5. What do you think the demons mean when they ask Jesus, "Have you come here to torment us before the time" (8:29)?

6. The Pharisees have problems with three things that Jesus and His disciples do in Mark 2:13–27. What three things do they accuse Him of? Are any of their accusations accurate? If so, which one(s)?

DAY 281 / JOHN 5

1. What kind of response does the lame man give when Jesus asks if he wants to be healed? How would you summarize his attitude?

2. Where does the lame man go after he's healed? Why do you think he goes to this place?

3. What problem do the Pharisees have with the healed man? What problem do the Pharisees have with Jesus?

4. Has Jesus broken the law by healing the man on the Sabbath? Why or why not?

5. According to Jesus, who has the role of judgment? Who assigned that role?

DAY 282 / MATTHEW 12; MARK 3; LUKE 6

1. What does Jesus say or imply is more important than the temple?

2. What does Jesus say or imply is more important than sacrifice?

3. According to Jesus, the purpose of the Sabbath is:

4. What do the members of Jesus's family think of His actions at this point?

5. How would you describe or define blasphemy against the Spirit (i.e., "the unpardonable sin")?

DAY 283 / MATTHEW 5–7

1. Look up the word "blessed" (5:3) in a Greek lexicon and write down what you find. What other meaning(s) does this word have?

2. In your own words, describe what it means to be "poor in spirit" or spiritually poor.

3. When reflecting on the Ten Commandments and other Old Testament laws in 5:17–48, what does Jesus repeatedly reveal about God's standards for holiness?

4. Look up the word "perfect" (5:48) in a Greek lexicon and write down what you find. What other meaning(s) does this word have?

5. Look up the word "judge" (7:1) in a Greek lexicon and write down what you find. What other meaning(s) does this word have?

6. Review 7:1–5, which warns against judging, then review 7:15–20, which seems to encourage it. On the surface, these two ideas seem to contradict each other, but how might they work together?

DAY 284 / MATTHEW 9; LUKE 7

1. What problem do the Pharisees have with Jesus's actions in 9:9–13? Summarize His response.

2. At what point in Jesus's interaction with the woman in 9:18–26 is she healed?

3. What prompts Jesus to heal the dead son in Nain? Who asks Him to heal him?

4. What can we infer about Jesus's power from Luke 7:39–40?

5. Rewrite Luke 7:47 in your own words.

DAY 285 / MATTHEW 11

1. John the Baptist is in prison, and he sends his followers to ask Jesus a question. What is the essence of his question? What emotion do you think is underneath this question?

2. How would you summarize Jesus's response to John the Baptist?

3. What do you think Jesus means by His words in 11:10–14? (See Malachi 3:1 and 4:5 for help.)

4. What happens to the cities that see Jesus perform the most miracles? Why?

5. According to Jesus's words in 11:27, what can we learn about the roles of the Father and the Son in the story of God's redemption of His kids?

DAY 286 / LUKE 11

1. Who does Jesus tell the disciples to address in their prayers?

2. Who does Jesus bless in 11:27–28?

3. Why does Jesus resist doing a miracle in front of the crowds who seek a sign (11:29–32)? What does this reveal about His motives in performing miracles?

4. When a Pharisee invites Jesus to dinner, he confronts Jesus about His hygiene. How would you describe Jesus's response to him?

5. How would you summarize Jesus's response to the lawyer who inserts himself into the conversation?

DAY 287 / MATTHEW 13; LUKE 8

1. Who is Jesus talking to when He tells the parable of the sower?

2. List the four places where the seed is sown in the parable of the sower. Beside each place, write what happens to the seed.

3. Underneath each type of soil, write a brief summary of the situation it represents in the parable (13:18–23).

4. Identify the following in the parable of the weeds: Who are the good seeds? Who are the weeds? Who are the reapers?

5. According to 13:55–56, how many brothers does Jesus have? How many sisters (at least) does He have?

6. In addition to the twelve apostles or disciples, who else traveled with Jesus as He preached throughout the region (8:1–3)? List them.

DAY 288 / MARK 4–5

1. In chapter 4, Jesus tells four parables back to back. What is the common theme that unites them?

2. Based on what you know so far, where or what is "the other side" in 4:35?

3. What powers did the man with the unclean spirit (5:1–20) get from the demons?

4. What other physical impacts did the demons have on him (5:5, 5:15)?

5. According to this story, what kind of relationship do the demons have to Jesus (see 5:6–7 and 5:13)?

DAY 289 / MATTHEW 10

1. Who does Jesus instruct the disciples to go to first? Why do you think He gives them this specific direction?

2. How does Jesus instruct them to respond if they encounter people who refuse to hear their message?

3. What kind of promise or warning does Jesus give them in 10:16–18?

4. Who will go with them to help prepare them to respond when accused?

5. According to Jesus in 10:26–33, what is the general theme of why the disciples shouldn't be afraid?

DAY 290 / MATTHEW 14; MARK 6; LUKE 9

1. Why had King Herod imprisoned John the Baptist?

2. When Herod gets word about Jesus and His words and actions, who does he think Jesus is? Why?

3. How do the apostles get power over demons and diseases? What does this reveal on a deeper level?

4. Compare the message of the apostles in Mark 6:12 and Luke 9:6. The messages may appear to be contradictory, but how might they actually work together?

5. Why do you think Scripture mentions specifically that there are twelve baskets left over after the loaves and fish have been multiplied to feed the people? Is there any significance in the five loaves and two fish?

DAY 291 / JOHN 6

1. How does Jesus respond to the people who have tracked Him down (6:25–27)?

2. Look up the word "believe" (6:29) in a Greek lexicon and write down what you find. What other meanings does this word have?

3. The crowd requests a miracle from Jesus, like when Moses gave them manna from heaven. What's ironic about this particular request?

4. What is Jesus's primary purpose on earth, according to 6:38–39?

5. Compare verses 37, 44–45, and 64–65. According to Jesus, how do we come to understand the gospel and draw near to God?

6. Compare verses 50–51 and 62. Where was Jesus before He was born in a manger?

DAY 292 / MATTHEW 15; MARK 7

1. The Pharisees claim that Jesus and His disciples are breaking the traditions of their elders. Are their claims correct? Why or why not? What does He accuse them of in return?

2. How many baskets are left over after Jesus feeds the crowd in 15:32–39? What's the significance of this number?

3. What grand declaration does Jesus make in 7:19? How does this shift things for His followers?

4. In 15:22, a Canaanite woman refers to Jesus as the "Son of David." What does this title mean, and what does it reveal about the woman who uses it?

5. What is the only thing Jesus is recorded as doing in Tyre and Sidon (7:24–30)?

DAY 293 / MATTHEW 16; MARK 8

1. What does the phrase "Son of Man" (16:13) mean? See Daniel 7:13 for help.

2. Look up the words "Peter" and "rock" (16:18) in a Greek lexicon and write down what you find. What other meanings does

each word have? How are these two words similar? How are they different?

3. What do you think Jesus means when He tells Peter He is giving him the "keys of the kingdom of heaven" (16:19)?

4. How would you summarize Jesus's statement to Peter in 16:23 and 8:33?

5. Why would Jesus use spit to heal the man's eyes when He could just as easily heal with a word or a thought (8:22–26)?

6. What might Jesus be trying to communicate by performing a partial healing followed by a complete healing, instead of an instantaneous healing?

DAY 294 / MATTHEW 17; MARK 9

1. Look up the word "transfigure" in a dictionary and write down what you find.

2. What does God the Father say about Jesus during His transfiguration? What instructions does the Father give to those who hear?

3. To whom does Jesus compare Elijah? What do the two have in common?

4. How does the demon impact the man's son? What does this reveal about the way demons treat the people they demonize?

5. Why does Jesus pay the temple tax, according to 17:27? What does this reveal about His values and priorities?

DAY 295 / MATTHEW 18

1. What attitudes and actions does Jesus connect with greatness?

2. Why do you think Jesus makes a habit of using children in His illustrations? How does this go against the cultural norms?

3. According to Jesus, where are the angels who are watching over the children?

4. What are the four steps in the process of confrontation listed in 18:15–17?

   1.

   2.

   3.

   4.

5. Review 18:17. Based on what you know so far, how does Jesus treat Gentiles (non-Jews) and tax collectors? Give examples from Scripture.

DAY 296 / JOHN 7–8

1. What do you think Jesus's brothers are trying to accomplish in 7:1–5?

2. Summarize the logic Jesus uses against the crowd in 7:21–23.

3. Review John 7:27. Are they referencing a prophecy from Scripture or a man-made tradition? (See 7:42 and Micah 5:2 for help.)

4. When Jesus is talking to the scribes and Pharisees in 8:38–47, He explains two different types of people. List out the various things that describe each type:
   A.

   B.

DAY 297 / JOHN 9–10

1. According to Jesus, why was the man born blind? Why is this challenging for the disciples to grasp?

2. What day is it when Jesus heals the blind man?

3. Why would Jesus make mud to put on the man's eyes instead of just speaking healing to the man?

4. List out the various ways the healed man describes Jesus throughout the story and notice how his descriptions evolve.

5. In chapter 10, what theme does Jesus repeat in verses 11, 15, 17, and 18? Why is this important to note?

6. Compare Jesus's words in 10:26–27 to His words in 8:42–47. What makes the difference between those who can hear and understand His words and those who can't?

1. The story in Luke 10:1–12 resembles the story in Matthew 10:5–15. If they're the same story, why might the numbers of people involved be different?

2. Compare Jesus's words in 10:18 to Isaiah 14:12, Ezekiel 28:11–19, and Revelation 20:1–10. What incident do you think He's describing to His disciples?

3. When the disciples rejoice that they have power over demons, Jesus tells them they're focusing on the wrong thing. What does He say they should rejoice about instead?

4. What legal loophole is the lawyer trying to find in his conversation with Jesus?

5. Based on Jesus's parable, who is your neighbor?

6. How would you summarize Jesus's words to Martha?

1. In the parable of the rich fool (12:13–21), it may appear at first that Jesus is condemning wealth and possessions, but what is He actually warning against?

2. When Peter asks Jesus if His words are for everyone or just for His followers (12:41), Jesus doesn't answer him directly, but His response seems to point Peter toward the answer. Who do you think Jesus's message is for and why?

3. In 13:1–5, the crowd has a question about some Jews who were killed; it seems they want to know why it happened. What does Jesus indicate in response to their question? What other more important point does He reiterate while they're on the topic?

4. In the parable of the fig tree, who is patient with the tree when it doesn't bear fruit? Who do you think the fig tree represents? Who do you think the gardener represents?

5. What kind of salvation do you think the man in 13:23 is referring to? Why?

6. How would you summarize the main points of Jesus's response to the man (13:24–30)?

DAY 300 / LUKE 14–15

1. Review 14:1–2. Given the Pharisees' disdain for people who have injuries or illness, why do you think this man with dropsy is in the home of a Pharisee on the Sabbath?

2. In the illustration Jesus uses in 14:18–20, what reasons do the people give for not attending the banquet? Is there anything objectively wrong with these reasons? What point is Jesus illustrating here?

3. According to 15:1–2, what kinds of people are drawn to Jesus? What kinds of people are repulsed by His actions?

4. Who is Jesus's audience for the trio of "lost" parables in chapter 15? Based on this information and the theme of the three parables, what message(s) do you think He's trying to communicate to the various audience members?

5. Look up the word "prodigal" in a standard dictionary and write down what you find.

DAY 301 / LUKE 16–17

1. According to 16:9, what does Jesus say will ultimately happen to "unrighteous wealth"? Is He telling them to seek it?

2. Review 16:16–17. Is Jesus saying the law has been abolished since John the Baptist came? Why or why not? If not, what is He communicating?

3. What aspects of 16:19–31 suggest that this could be a true story instead of a parable? Which do you think it is? Why?

4. How would you summarize the point of 16:31?

5. Who is Jesus talking to in 17:20–21? What bearing does this have on the meaning of His words here? What is Jesus revealing to them?

DAY 302 / JOHN 11

1. According to Jesus, why is Lazarus sick, and what will be the end result of his illness?

2. Visual search: Look up the village of Bethany on a map of ancient Israel. Find where it is located in relation to Jerusalem (see 11:18).

3. What is the first thing Martha says to Jesus? How does He respond to her?

4. What is the first thing Mary says to Jesus? How does He respond to her?

5. What do some of the Jews fear will happen if Jesus keeps doing these things?

6. What two major things is Caiaphas pointing to in 11:49–52?

DAY 303 / LUKE 18

1. Is Jesus making a direct comparison between God and the wicked judge? What is His primary message?

2. Who is Jesus talking to when He tells the parable about the Pharisee and the tax collector (look back to 17:20)? What point is He making to His audience?

3. How would you describe the tone of the Pharisee's prayer? How would you describe the tone of the tax collector's prayer?

4. Which of the commandments does Jesus quote to the rich ruler? What theme unites these particular commandments?

5. Is the rich ruler accurate in saying he has kept all of God's laws? Why or why not? What does this reveal about his heart?

6. When Jesus responds, what offer does He make the rich ruler?

DAY 304 / MATTHEW 19; MARK 10

1. Summarize each section of the Pharisees' conversation with Jesus in 19:1–9.

    A. Question (19:3):

    B. Answer (19:4–6):

    C. Question (19:7):

    D. Answer (19:8–9):

2. In 19:10, the disciples say Jesus's teaching on divorce is challenging. What alternative do they suggest, and how does Jesus respond?

3. According to 10:16, what is the purpose of laying hands on someone when you pray for them? Do you think its purpose is more functional or symbolic?

4. Do James and John get what they ask Jesus for? Why or why not?

5. Rewrite Mark 10:45 in your own words.

DAY 305 / MATTHEW 20–21

1. How would you summarize the main theme of Jesus's parable in 20:1–16?

2. According to 20:18–19, what groups of people will be involved in Jesus's arrest, condemnation, and death? How are these groups similar? How are they different? Why is it noteworthy that both groups are involved?

3. Look up the word "hosanna" (21:9) in a Greek lexicon and write down what you find. What do you think the people are asking Jesus to do by calling out this phrase to Him?

4. Why do you think Jesus curses the fig tree? Review Luke 13:6–9 for help.

5. Who do the two sons represent in 21:28–31 (see 21:32)? What's the general message Jesus is sending in this parable?

DAY 306 / LUKE 19

1. Visual search: Locate Jericho on a map of Israel and look up its distance from Jerusalem.

2. Compare and contrast Zaccheus with the rich ruler in Luke 18:18–30.

3. Rewrite Luke 19:10 in your own words.

4. Why does Jesus weep over Jerusalem?

1. Read Zechariah 9:9. How many years prior to Jesus's triumphal entry into Jerusalem was this prophecy written? Use a study Bible or do a web search for help.

2. What role does Judas fill among the apostles?

3. According to 12:37–40, why are the people unable to believe in Jesus despite all His signs?

4. Who is the "ruler of this world" referenced in 12:31? For possible help, use a study Bible or see 2 Corinthians 4:4.

5. In 12:49–50, whose authority and plan is Jesus submitting to? According to 12:50, what is the plan?

1. What similarities do you notice between the parable of the wedding feast and the story Jesus told just prior to this in the parable of the tenants (Matthew 21:33–46 and Mark 12:1–12)? What point is Jesus trying to drive home for the chief priests and the Pharisees who are listening to both parables?

2. How is the temple tax (Matthew 17:24–27) different from the taxes paid to Caesar? What message does Jesus send about paying taxes to Caesar?

3. What doctrine (teaching, belief) of Scripture do the Sadducees reject? How do they use their beliefs to try to trap Jesus?

4. What two commands does Jesus use to summarize all the laws of the Old Testament? Is He eliminating any laws by reducing them to these two? Why or why not?

5. What is Jesus quoting in 22:44? What does He confirm about the authorship of this passage? Why is this important?

DAY 309 / MATTHEW 23; LUKE 20–21

1. What do you think Jesus means by His command in 23:9?

2. Visual search: Do a web search for an image of a phylactery. Review Deuteronomy 11:18. Based on this verse, what purpose do you think phylacteries serve?

3. In your Bible, underline the word "woe" each time it appears in 23:13–36, or write the references below. Then briefly summarize each of the seven woes.

4. Look up the phrase "equal to angels" (20:36) in a Greek lexicon and write down what you find. What does this verse seem to be saying? What is it not saying?

5. Who is Jesus speaking to in 21:10–19? Why is it important to note His audience?

6. How can we reconcile Jesus's words in 21:16 with His words in 21:18–19?

DAY 310 / MARK 13

1. In what year was Jesus's prophecy of temple destruction fulfilled? Use a study Bible or do a web search for help.

2. Who specifically is Jesus talking to in 13:3–37? Why is it important to note His audience?

3. What instructions does Jesus repeat to this group of apostles in both 13:7 and 13:11?

4. What instructions does Jesus repeat to this group of apostles in 13:33, 35, and 37?

5. In today's reading, Jesus gives His apostles information and instructions. How would you summarize His words to them?

DAY 311 / MATTHEW 24

1. Who specifically is Jesus talking to in 24:3–51 (see Mark 13:3 for help)? Why is it important to note His audience?

2. According to 24:22, why does God keep this period of trials short?

3. Review 24:29. Do you believe this verse points to a literal or symbolic occurrence? What do you think it means?

4. After Jesus returns, from where will the elect be gathered (see also Mark 13:27)?

5. What does Jesus mean in 24:34? How can we reconcile His words here with His words in 24:36?

DAY 312 / MATTHEW 25

1. What does oil often symbolize in Scripture? How does that pertain to the meaning of the parable of the ten virgins?

2. How would you summarize the main message of the parable of the ten virgins?

3. Look up the word "talent" (25:15) in a Greek lexicon and write down what you find. How does 25:18 help clarify which definition applies?

4. Why doesn't the third servant invest his money and use it wisely? Is his view of the master accurate? Why or why not?

5. How would you summarize the main message of the parable of the talents?

6. What has God prepared for the sheep, according to 25:34? What has God prepared for the goats, according to 25:41? Who else is included in what the goats receive?

DAY 313 / MATTHEW 26; MARK 14

1. What are some of the specific details Jesus knows and reveals about His death in 26:1–2?

2. Based on the timing of Judas's plotting in 26:14–16, how might the previous incident in 26:6–13 have played a role in his decision?

3. In 26:22–25, how is Judas's question different from the question the other apostles ask? What significance does this hold?

4. In 26:26–29, what items are mentioned as a part of their Passover meal?

DAY 314 / LUKE 22; JOHN 13

1. Look up the word "demanded" (22:31) in a Greek lexicon and write down what you find. What does this reveal about the tone of the exchange between Jesus and Satan?

2. According to Luke 22, at what point does Satan enter into Judas? How does this vary from the account in John 13? How could these accounts work together?

3. How would you summarize the point Jesus is making in 22:35–38? Why would He tell them to get a sword? (Use a study Bible or commentary for help.)

4. Jesus says He is giving them a "new" commandment in 13:34–35. How is this command different from what He's been telling them all along?

5. If Jesus is fully God, how could He have a desire that stands in contrast to the will of the Father (22:42)?

6. What is the practical purpose of foot washing? What is the spiritual reality Jesus is pointing to through foot washing?

DAY 315 / JOHN 14–17

1. What does Jesus mean in 14:7? See Colossians 1:15 and Hebrews 1:3 for help. How does this help shape our understanding of God

the Father? How does this help carry the thread of the storyline from Old Testament to New Testament with consistency?

2. Look up the word "greater" (14:12) in a Greek lexicon and write down what you find. What possible definitions might apply here, especially considering His use of the word "because" afterward?

3. What does it mean to ask for something "in Jesus's name" (14:13–14)? How does 16:23–24 help fill out our understanding of this statement?

4. What does Jesus mean when He says it's to their advantage that He goes away (16:7)? How is the Holy Spirit a greater advantage to them than Jesus?

5. What are some of the roles of the Holy Spirit that Jesus emphasizes and uses to encourage and embolden His disciples (see 14:17, 14:26, 15:26, 16:7–15)?

DAY 316 / MATTHEW 27; MARK 15

1. Review Leviticus 16:6–10. How does this story point toward what happens with Barabbas in today's reading?

2. According to Revelation 13:8, for how long has the plan of Jesus being slain for our sins been set in motion?

3. Read Matthew 27:3–5 and compare it with 2 Corinthians 7:10. Which of the two perspectives described in 7:10 represents Judas here?

4. According to 27:18 and 15:10, why do the chief priests want Jesus to be killed?

5. What strange event is recorded in Matthew 27:52–53? What does this demonstrate or symbolize?

DAY 317 / LUKE 23; JOHN 18–19

1. What accusations do the people make against Jesus when they present Him to the Roman governor, Pontius Pilate?

2. What does Herod find Jesus guilty of? What does Pilate find Jesus guilty of?

3. Review Isaiah 52:14. What does this tell us about the severity of the beatings Jesus received?

4. Who specifically does Jesus ask the Father to forgive? Why do you think He doesn't ask the Father to forgive everyone involved, including people like Herod, Pilate, the chief priests, or Judas?

5. Review 23:43. Based on this passage, where does it seem like Jesus is going when He dies? What other verses in Scripture point to His destination during the three days between His crucifixion and His resurrection?

1. Who seems most frightened by the angel? Who is the angel addressing when he says, "Do not be afraid"? What's noteworthy about this distinction?

2. Why do you think Mary doesn't recognize Jesus at first? What practical factors may contribute to this? When does she recognize Him?

3. What instructions does Jesus give Mary in 28:10? Review Matthew 26:31. What do you think the disciples expect to hear from Him, based on this?

4. What command does Jesus give the apostles in 28:18–20?

5. What promise does Jesus give them in 28:18–20?

1. Why don't the men on the road to Emmaus recognize Jesus? What causes the men to finally recognize Him? What happens to Jesus after they recognize Him?

2. In His conversation with the men, what word does Jesus use to describe His own death and crucifixion?

3. Why is it important to note that Jesus ate food?

4. What's noteworthy about the fact that the face cloth is folded up and set aside? What important information does this reveal to Peter and John?

5. According to 20:12, where are the two angels located? Compare this with Exodus 25:22. What do you notice?

6. Look up the two uses of "love" (21:15) in a Greek lexicon and write down what you find. What's significant about the word Jesus uses versus the word Peter uses? How does Jesus's word choice

change by the third time He asks the question in 21:17? What are your thoughts about the implications of this transition?

DAY 320 / ACTS 1–3

1. Who wrote Acts?

2. To or for whom was it written?

3. When was it written?

4. What is the literary style (narrative, history, wisdom, prophecy, letter, etc.)?

5. List the people who meet regularly in the upper room. What's noteworthy about this list? Are there any people you wouldn't expect to see included?

6. Look up the word "tongues" (2:4) in a Greek lexicon and write down what you find. Which definitions suit the context?

7. Why would speaking in other languages be helpful for them? Consider the immediate context of 2:5.

8. What is the crux of Peter's message on the day of Pentecost?

DAY 321 / ACTS 4–6

1. After Peter and John are released from prison, what is their primary prayer request (4:23–30)? What does this reveal about their primary purpose?

2. What two possible courses of action could Ananias and Sapphira have taken that wouldn't have incited condemnation?

3. According to 5:15, what rumor seems to spread about Peter's healing abilities? Does Scripture confirm or deny the merit of this rumor?

4. How would you summarize Gamaliel's advice to the religious leaders?

5. In 5:17–42, the apostles are arrested, beaten, and released. According to 5:41, why do they rejoice? What does this reveal about their primary purpose?

6. Who are the Hellenists? What problem are they experiencing? How does the early church work together to solve that problem?

DAY 322 / ACTS 7–8

1. Look up the phrase "host of heaven" (7:42) in a Greek lexicon and write down what you find. Based on the possible definitions and the context of 7:40–43, what does it seem the people were worshipping?

2. What is Stephen's accusation against the forefathers of the Sanhedrin? What is his accusation against the members of the Sanhedrin themselves?

3. How does Scripture describe Jesus in 7:55–56? What's noteworthy about this?

4. At whose feet do the Sanhedrin throw their cloaks when they're preparing to stone Stephen?

5. When Philip flees Jerusalem, where does he go to preach the gospel? Why do some people have a hard time believing in the conversion of the people in this particular region?

DAY 323 / ACTS 9–10

1. According to 9:2, what term is used to describe the early church at this point in its history?

2. Who does Jesus accuse Saul of persecuting in 9:4–5? What's noteworthy about this?

3. According to Ananias in 9:13, who is Saul persecuting?

4. How do locals in Damascus respond when they hear about Saul's conversion? How do the people in Jerusalem respond? Who is the one person who responds differently?

5. What spiritual truth is God communicating to Peter through his rooftop vision?

1. Who is especially displeased with Peter's vision and the results of it? What do they think should be done instead? Why?

2. Who does the church have to look to for guidance and direction as they make adjustments and spread the gospel to new cultures?

3. Who does Peter quote when he convinces the circumcision party that his actions were justified? What did that person say that pertains to the matter at hand?

4. In what city is the early church first collectively referred to as "Christians"?

5. How does the apostle James die?

6. What happens to the prison guards who are working when the angel helps Peter escape?

7. Who joins Saul and Barnabas as they head back to Antioch?

DAY 325 / ACTS 13–14

1. Who does Manaen work for? What's noteworthy about this?

2. What two names or titles does Saul use when referring to Bar-Jesus?

3. Why might Saul start being referred to as Paul, the Gentile version of his name, at this point in the story?

4. How would you summarize Paul's encouragement to the people in the synagogue in Antioch (13:16–41)?

5. On their second visit to the synagogue in Antioch (13:44–52), who begins to be drawn in by Paul's message? Who begins to resist Paul's message? What do you think accounts for these different responses?

6. Who shows up to attack Paul in Lystra? How does he respond afterward?

DAY 326 / JAMES 1–5

1. Who wrote James?

2. To or for whom was it written?

3. When was it written?

4. What is the literary style (narrative, history, wisdom, prophecy, letter, etc.)?

5. Look up the word "perfect" (1:4) in a Greek lexicon and write down what you find. What other meaning(s) does this word have? In the original language, how many times is that word used in this verse?

6. Look up the word "justified" (2:24) in a Greek lexicon and write down what you find. How might that information shape our understanding of this verse? Is James saying our works save us?

7. According to 3:17, what does God-given wisdom look like?

8. How would you summarize the overarching theme of the book of James?

DAY 327 / ACTS 15–16

1. What have the people from the church in Jerusalem begun teaching at the new church plant in Antioch? Who has stirred up the trouble? Are these people Christ followers? (See 15:5 for help.)

2. When James speaks up, he points to an Old Testament prophecy from Amos. Summarize the message of the prophecy he references in 15:16–18.

3. Why does Paul refuse to let John Mark join them on their visit to the churches they planted? See Acts 13:13 for help.

4. Why would Paul have Timothy circumcised? This seems to contradict his prior message on circumcision, but how might it actually be consistent with a broader message he has communicated?

5. What do Paul and Silas do after being released from prison and preaching the gospel to the jailer's family? Why?

DAY 328 / GALATIANS 1–3

1. Who wrote Galatians?

2. To or for whom was it written?

3. When was it written?

4. What is the literary style (narrative, history, wisdom, prophecy, letter, etc.)?

5. Which minister did the church send primarily to the Gentiles? Which minister did the church send primarily to the Jews?

6. For what offense or sin did Paul have to confront Peter (also called Cephas) about?

7. How would you summarize the message Paul repeats in 2:16, 2:21, 3:3, and 3:10?

8. How would you summarize the message Paul repeats in 3:7 and 3:29?

DAY 329 / GALATIANS 4–6

1. Review 4:8–11. What do you think Paul is referring to when he rebukes the Galatians in verse 10? Use a study Bible for help.

2. Considering the context, what does Paul mean when he tells the Galatians not to submit to a yoke of slavery again (5:1)?

3. Rewrite 5:4 in your own words.

4. Write out the list of the works of the flesh in 5:19–21. Then write out the list of the fruit of the Spirit in 5:22–23. For each work of the flesh, identify an aspect of the Spirit's fruit that speaks to the core problem.

5. How would you summarize the overarching theme of Paul's letter to the Galatians?

DAY 330 / ACTS 17

1. What does Paul use as the basis for his discussion and persuasion in Thessalonica?

2. Who believes Paul's message? Who doesn't?

3. What do the Bereans do in response to Paul's teaching each day?

4. How does 17:16 describe Athens? How does that set Athens apart from the other places where Paul has gone to preach?

5. Paul has been using Scripture to reason with the people in the synagogues in other cities. How does he shift his approach when preaching to the Athenians? See 17:28 for help.

DAY 331 / 1 THESSALONIANS 1–5; 2 THESSALONIANS 1–3

1. Who wrote 1 and 2 Thessalonians?

2. To or for whom were they written?

3. When were they written?

4. What is the literary style (narrative, history, wisdom, prophecy, letter, etc.)?

5. According to 1 Thessalonians 1:4–10, what three or four proofs does Paul cite as evidence that God loves the people of Thessalonica and has made them His own?

6. What two things does Paul clearly state as "God's will" in 1 Thessalonians?

7. Look up the word "sanctified" in a dictionary and write down what you find. According to 1 Thessalonians 5:23, how and by whom are we sanctified?

8. Look up the word "temple" (2 Thessalonians 2:4) in a Greek lexicon and write down what you find. What variety of buildings are described by this term?

DAY 332 / ACTS 18–19

1. What does Paul's act of shaking out his garments symbolize? Is he directing this toward all Jews or only the Jews in Corinth? How do you know?

2. What does 18:18 tell us about Paul's time in Corinth? What vow has Paul likely taken? Why do you think he takes this vow while in Corinth?

3. Review 18:24–19:7. What belief had these baptized people affirmed prior to meeting Paul, Aquila, and Priscilla? How does Jesus's coming to earth, dying, and resurrecting change the landscape of what they had affirmed?

4. What lessons can we learn from the seven brothers who try to treat Jesus's name like an incantation against a demon?

5. On what basis does the silversmith dismiss the gospel Paul is preaching?

DAY 333 / 1 CORINTHIANS 1–4

1. Who wrote 1 Corinthians?

2. To or for whom was it written?

3. When was it written?

4. What is the literary style (narrative, history, wisdom, prophecy, letter, etc.)?

5. Rewrite 1:18 in your own words.

6. How would you summarize the theme of 2:10–16?

DAY 334 / 1 CORINTHIANS 5–8

1. How does the church at Corinth seem to view their sexual exploits prior to this letter from Paul? In what ways have they misunderstood grace and what it means to be free in Christ? Compare Paul's response to them here with his words to other believers in Romans 6:1 and Galatians 5:13.

2. Under what circumstances does Paul say to "deliver someone over to Satan" in 5:4–5? And for what purpose?

3. How would you summarize Paul's words in 5:11–12?

4. Does Paul forbid lawsuits among believers? What alternative does he suggest?

5. Visual search: In chapter 7, Paul is careful to delineate between his own opinions and God's instructions. To help understand the distinctions better, underline every place in chapter 7 where Paul

clarifies that a statement is his own opinion ("I say," "I wish," "I want," "I give this charge," "in my judgment," etc.). Then, circle every place where Paul clarifies that the instructions are directly from God ("not I, but the Lord," "the Lord has assigned," etc.).

6. How would you summarize the problem in chapter 8? How would you summarize Paul's guidance to them?

DAY 335 / 1 CORINTHIANS 9–11

1. Why has Paul chosen not to receive financial support from the church at Corinth, even though he has a right to it?

2. What does Paul mean when he says, "I have become all things to all people, that by all means I might save some" (9:22)?

3. In chapter 10, Paul recounts God's history of faithfulness to His people. What are some of the aspects of God's character that he focuses on in this chapter?

4. How might Paul's focus on God's character serve to draw the Corinthians away from their idolatry problem?

5. Review 10:25–30. Under what circumstances does Paul say it is acceptable for believers to eat food sacrificed to idols? Under what circumstances does he say it's unwise or unloving for believers to eat food sacrificed to idols?

6. Which "body" do you think Paul is referring to in 11:29? Why?

DAY 336 / 1 CORINTHIANS 12–14

1. According to 12:7, what is the purpose of spiritual gifts?

2. Based on chapter 13, what is the danger in using our gifts for anything other than this purpose? What is the danger in using our gifts without love and service as the motivator?

3. What do you think Paul means in 12:31? How might this intersect with his words in 14:1–5? On what basis are some gifts considered higher than others?

4. Why is love greater than faith and hope? What does this mean? What does it not mean?

5. How can we reconcile Paul's words in 14:34–35 with his words in 11:5 and 11:13?

DAY 337 / 1 CORINTHIANS 15–16

1. What doctrine (belief about God) do the Corinthians seem to be struggling with in chapter 15? How is this doctrine foundational to our faith?

2. What do you think Paul means by his words in 15:29? Use a study Bible for help. Is this text descriptive or prescriptive?

3. What impact has their disbelief in the resurrection had on their lives?

4. On what day of the week does Paul collect money from the church to send to those in need? What might this indicate about the practices of the early church?

DAY 338 / 2 CORINTHIANS 1–4

1. Who wrote 2 Corinthians?

2. To or for whom was it written?

3. When was it written?

4. What is the literary style (narrative, history, wisdom, prophecy, letter, etc.)?

5. List out the four things Paul attributes to God in 1:21–22.

6. According to 2:14–16, what are the two possible responses to the aroma of the gospel of Christ?

DAY 339 / 2 CORINTHIANS 5–9

1. What do you think Paul means in 2 Corinthians 5:1–4? Does this point to our future selves (in the new heavens and the new earth) being disembodied spirits or embodied spirits? Based on your current understanding, describe the state of those who are currently in heaven, and describe how that state might change after Christ's return to earth. Use a study Bible for help and cite Scripture when possible.

2. Review 5:16–20. What does it mean that we are "ministers of reconciliation"? To whom are we called to minister?

3. Do a web search for an image of a yoke. How does this help frame your understanding of Paul's instructions in 6:14–7:1?

4. What theme does Paul point to in 6:10, 7:4, and 8:2?

5. How would you summarize the theme of Paul's message in 8:1–15?

DAY 340 / 2 CORINTHIANS 10–13

1. According to 10:2, what has Paul been accused of? How does he defend himself?

2. Who are the "super-apostles" Paul refers to in 11:5? Use a study Bible for help.

3. Why are the Corinthians swayed by the message of the super-apostles instead of Paul's message?

4. What do you think Paul means when he references the "third heaven"? Use a study Bible for help.

5. How does Paul describe his thorn in the flesh? What do you think it is? What happens when Paul asks God to remove it? What reason does God give for responding the way He does?

DAY 341 / ROMANS 1–3

1. Who wrote Romans?

2. To or for whom was it written?

3. When was it written?

4. What is the literary style (narrative, history, wisdom, prophecy, letter, etc.)?

5. Three times in chapter 1, Paul says, "God gave them up." What actions preceded this response each time?

6. Review the list in 1:29–30. Which things on this list feel tame to you by comparison? Is it shocking that verse 32 says these things warrant death? What does this reveal about God's standards for holiness?

7. In your Bible, circle every use of the phrase "by faith" or "through faith" in 3:21–31. What is the theme of Paul's message here?

DAY 342 / ROMANS 4–7

1. Why does Paul choose Abraham as an example of salvation by faith, as opposed to the works of the law? How many years did Abraham live prior to the establishment of the law through Moses? Do a web search for help.

2. Abraham lived long before the law was given, but God commanded him to be set apart through circumcision. Did he receive salvation through his obedience to this command? Why or why not?

3. According to 5:3–5, what does suffering produce in us? Why are these things important?

4. In 5:12–21, circle every use of "much more," "all the more," and "abundance" (or similar phrases) in your Bible, or write the references here. Review each verse. What does this theme reveal about God's character?

5. How would you summarize Paul's message in 6:19?

6. What analogies have been helpful for you in understanding the distinct roles of the law and the gospel? If you can't recall any, try to form an analogy and write it here.

DAY 343 / ROMANS 8–10

1. Rewrite 8:1 in your own words. What does the word "therefore" point us back to?

2. In the sections below, list the things 8:5–17 associates with both options.

Flesh:

Spirit:

3. Paul knows his words in 9:1–13 will be hard for his readers. What questions or problems does he assume they will have, based on 9:14 and 9:19? What responses does he offer?

4. In 9:22–23, what aspects of God's character does Paul suggest that He's trying to "show" and "make known"?

5. Based on the hope of Romans 8 and the big picture of Romans 9, what does Paul encourage his readers to do in 10:14–15?

DAY 344 / ROMANS 11–13

1. Since Paul has been making the point that anyone who has the Spirit is a child of Abraham, regardless of nationality, he makes a concerted effort to address ethnic Israel in chapter 11. How would you summarize his words to them?

2. What words of caution does Paul speak to the Gentile believers in chapter 11?

3. What two aspects of God's character does Paul point to in the cutting and grafting process of the branches (11:22)? Why is it important to be mindful of both?

4. What do you think Paul means when he says "all Israel" will be saved (11:25–26)? Explain your view and/or cite Scripture.

5. What guidance does Paul give in chapter 12 for discerning God's will?

6. How does chapter 13 inform our response to those God has placed in authority in our lives?

DAY 345 / ROMANS 14–16

1. What kinds of things does Paul say believers shouldn't quarrel over? Why?

2. Look up the word used for "keep" (14:22) in a Greek lexicon and write down what you find. How does this help inform our understanding of this verse?

3. What is Paul referring to in 15:4? Rewrite this verse in your own words.

4. In 15:8–13, Paul cites four different passages from the Old Testament. What theme do they have in common? Why do you think Paul is making this point here?

5. Look up the word "servant" (16:1) in a Greek lexicon and write down what you find. How does this help develop our understanding of Paul's views on women?

DAY 346 / ACTS 20–23

1. According to 20:22–24, what does the Spirit keep reminding Paul about? Does Paul seem to receive this information as a deterrent or a means of preparation?

2. In 20:28–35, what two things does Paul make sure to remind the Ephesians of before he leaves?

3. Review 20:22, then read 21:4. How might these two verses work together?

4. When Agabus prophesies, does he give Paul instruction or information?

5. Why does James think it would be wise for Paul to join some of the locals in their vow?

6. At what point in Paul's defense before the Jews do they grow angry and begin to riot and demand his death? What does this reveal about their understanding of the gospel?

DAY 347 / ACTS 24–26

1. What are the primary things Tertullus accuses Paul of in 24:5–6? Is Paul guilty of these things?

2. According to 24:26, why does Felix repeatedly summon Paul to share the gospel with him?

3. Review 26:18. When someone's eyes are opened to the truth of the gospel, what two things do they turn from and what four things do they gain?

4. Rewrite 26:29 in your own words.

DAY 348 / ACTS 27–28

1. Is it immediately clear whether Paul's first words of guidance in 27:9–10 are from God or from Paul? If so, who is the guidance from? If not, when and how does it become clear?

2. In what ways does Paul demonstrate God's power and goodness among the Romans and prisoners on the ship?

3. In what ways does Paul demonstrate God's power and goodness on the island of Malta?

4. What series of events shifts the way the locals in Malta view Paul?

5. When it comes to Jews and Gentiles, what is the typical order of Paul's ministry focus in each new location? Why do you think that is?

DAY 349 / COLOSSIANS 1–4; PHILEMON 1

1. Who wrote Colossians and Philemon?

2. To or for whom were they written?

3. When were they written?

4. What is the literary style (narrative, history, wisdom, prophecy, letter, etc.)?

5. According to Colossians 1:21–23, what serves as evidence that we have been reconciled to God?

6. According to 2:16–23, what are the two primary ways the church at Colossae is prone to deception?

7. In the book of Philemon, who is Onesimus and what has he done?

8. How would you describe Paul's attitude toward Onesimus? Toward Philemon?

DAY 350 / EPHESIANS 1–6

1. Who wrote Ephesians?

2. To or for whom was it written?

3. When was it written?

4. What is the literary style (narrative, history, wisdom, prophecy, letter, etc.)?

5. In 1:3–14, Paul lists many of the things God has done in the story of our salvation. According to verse 3, when did He set this plan into motion? How does this timing serve to help us fill out our view of God?

6. In 2:11–22, Paul speaks directly about the way the Gentiles' background as non-Jews connects with God's grace. How would you summarize his message in this section?

7. What two types of reconciliation are happening in 2:16–22?

DAY 351 / PHILIPPIANS 1–4

1. Who wrote Philippians?

2. To or for whom was it written?

3. When was it written?

4. What is the literary style (narrative, history, wisdom, prophecy, letter, etc.)?

5. What theme does Paul repeat in 1:6 and 2:12–13?

6. According to 1:29, what two things have been granted to the church? Why do you think Paul finds it necessary to remind them of this?

1. Who wrote 1 Timothy and 2 Timothy?

2. To or for whom were they written?

3. When were they written?

4. What is the literary style (narrative, history, wisdom, prophecy, letter, etc.)?

5. Review 2:13–15. What do you think Paul means in verse 15? Use a study Bible for help.

6. Review the list of qualifications for elders, or overseers, in 3:1–7. Are these things primarily related to skill set or to character?

7. In general, how are the qualifications for deacons different from the qualifications for elders?

8. What do you think Paul means in 4:10? Use a study Bible for help.

DAY 353 / TITUS 1–3

1. Who wrote Titus?

2. To or for whom was it written?

3. When was it written?

4. What is the literary style (narrative, history, wisdom, prophecy, letter, etc.)?

5. According to 1:1–2, what four things is Paul hoping to impart to the church at Crete or remind them about?

6. What challenges of false doctrine is Titus facing within the church?

7. What cultural challenges is Titus facing in Crete that are impacting the people in the church? What is Paul's counsel for addressing this problem?

DAY 354 / 1 PETER 1–5

1. Who wrote 1 Peter and 2 Peter?

2. To or for whom were they written?

3. When were they written?

4. What is the literary style (narrative, history, wisdom, prophecy, letter, etc.)?

5. According to 2:5 and 2:9, what title do believers hold? How can knowing our identity help us to live with wisdom and holiness in the midst of trials?

6. In 3:14–16, what are the four things Peter says believers should do when they're suffering for the sake of righteousness?

7. What does Peter mean in 3:21? Is he preaching salvation by works? Why or why not? Use a study Bible for help.

DAY 355 / HEBREWS 1–6

1. Who wrote Hebrews?

2. To or for whom was it written?

3. When was it written?

4. What is the literary style (narrative, history, wisdom, prophecy, letter, etc.)?

5. According to 1:10–12, what two places will perish? What or who will not perish?

6. What is the purpose of God's angels, according to 1:14?

7. How would you summarize the author's message in 3:14?

8. Although we are priests (1 Peter 2:5, 2:9), what are the implications of having Jesus as our high priest, according to 4:14–16?

DAY 356 / HEBREWS 7–10

1. Review the story of Melchizedek in Genesis 14:18–20. What similarities do you notice between him and Jesus?

2. According to 7:23–28, why is it better for us to be under a new covenant with Jesus as our high priest? List as many reasons as you can find.

3. If 10:4 is true, then why did God set up the sacrificial system in the Old Testament?

4. What theme does the author repeat in 9:26, 10:12, and 10:14?

DAY 357 / HEBREWS 11–13

1. According to 11:2, how did the people we read about in the Old Testament come into a relationship with God? Was their salvation by works?

2. Based on the stories of the people listed in the "Hall of Faith" in chapter 11, does our faith entitle us to easy lives and getting a "yes" to all our prayers? How does 11:3–40 guard us against taking 11:1 out of context?

3. What does 11:39 mean? Was God unfaithful to His promise? Why or why not?

4. According to 12:11, what are the benefits of discipline?

DAY 358 / 2 TIMOTHY 1–4

1. According to 1:6–7, what is the natural response we'll face if we don't engage with the faith God has given us? What is the spiritual response we'll face if we do?

2. According to 1:8–9, what is not the reason God saved us? What is the reason God saved us? What does this reveal about God?

3. Considering the context of 2:14–26, what do you think Paul is referring to when he tells Timothy to "flee youthful passions"?

4. What promise do we see in 3:12?

5. Review 3:16–17, then fill in the three sections below as they correspond to this passage:

A. What does God do?

B. What does God do through Scripture?

C. What does God do in us through Scripture?

DAY 359 / 2 PETER 1–3; JUDE 1

1. According to 2 Peter 1:5–7, what are the seven traits Peter wants to see growing in believers? What is the result of that growth, according to 1:8?

2. According to 2 Peter 2:4, what happens to the angels who sin?

3. Who wrote Jude?

4. To or for whom was it written?

5. When was it written?

6. What is the literary style (narrative, history, wisdom, prophecy, letter, etc.)?

7. According to Jude 1:8–9, what happened after Moses died? What might the devil stand to gain from this?

8. How did the archangel Michael respond in that situation?

DAY 360 / 1 JOHN 1–5

1. Who wrote 1 John, 2 John, and 3 John?

2. To or for whom were they written?

3. When were they written?

4. What is the literary style (narrative, history, wisdom, prophecy, letter, etc.)?

5. Look up the word "antichrist" (2:18) in a Greek lexicon and write down what you find. Compare this verse and definition with Jesus's words in Matthew 12:30. What makes someone an antichrist?

6. According to 2:19, why will those who ultimately walk away from their relationship with God and His church do so?

7. Who are the three witnesses John calls in chapter 5? Briefly explain each. Use a study Bible for help.

8. Rewrite 5:14–15 in your own words.

DAY 361 / 2 JOHN 1; 3 JOHN 1

1. Who is "the elect lady" in 2 John 1:1?

2. What are the two primary themes of 2 John? How do they tie together?

3. According to 2 John 1:9, what is the evidence that someone is a part of God's family?

4. Though Gaius doesn't appear to be a preacher or teacher, John says he's serving in an important role as a "fellow worker" in 3 John 1:8. What is his role?

DAY 362 / REVELATION 1–5

1. Who wrote Revelation?

2. To or for whom was it written?

3. When was it written?

4. What is the literary style (narrative, history, wisdom, prophecy, letter, etc.)?

5. What does the number seven symbolize in Jewish culture?

6. Which churches does Jesus call to repent? Why doesn't He call the others to repent?

7. According to 5:10, when we reign with Christ, where will we reign?

DAY 363 / REVELATION 6–11

1. With each of the first four seals, who calls for the horses to come out? What does this reveal about the role of the horses and the riders in God's plan?

2. According to 6:4 and 6:8, the riders are "permitted" and "given authority." What does this indicate about their position to God?

3. What will believers have on their foreheads (9:4)?

4. According to 9:20–21, what is the result for those who survive the plagues of God's wrath? Why do you think this is the case? Where else have we seen this happen in Scripture?

5. Review 10:5–6. Describe the angel's stance. Given the context, what might this position symbolize?

6. Based on the powers mentioned in 11:5–6, what two people from Scripture do you think might be referenced or imaged here?

DAY 364 / REVELATION 12–18

1. Chapter 12 is filled with signs and symbols. Based on what you know about Israel's history, who do you think the early church would perceive to be the "woman"? Why?

2. What happens when Satan and his angels are cast from heaven? Where are they sent?

3. Who do you think the early church would perceive to be the "beast" in 13:1–10? In their time, who could rightly be described by the words "the whole earth marveled as they followed the beast" (13:3)? Why?

4. Who gave the beast its authority? What is noteworthy about this?

5. In what ways does the second beast counterfeit the story of Jesus and His people?

6. Who do you think the early church would perceive to be the "woman" in Revelation 17? Why?

DAY 365 / REVELATION 19–22

1. For what action is John rebuked in chapter 19?

2. Compare 19:8 with 19:14. Which people seem to be enlisted in "the armies of heaven"?

3. What is the ultimate destination for Satan and his angels? According to 20:14–15, who else joins them there?

4. According to chapter 21, specifically verses 1–2 and 10, what seems to be the eternal dwelling place for God and His people?

5. Why is there no temple in the new Jerusalem?

6. What does Jesus reiterate three times in chapter 22?

About the Author

Tara-Leigh Cobble's zeal for biblical literacy led her to create D-Group (Discipleship Group), which has grown into an international network of three hundred–plus Bible study groups that meet every week in homes, in churches, and online. She also writes and hosts a daily radio show called *The God Shot*, as well as a daily podcast called *The Bible Recap*, which unpacks the richness of Scripture alongside the chronological one-year reading plan. In just over two years, the podcast garnered 70 million downloads and reached number three on the Apple Podcast Top Overall Charts. More than twenty thousand churches around the world have joined the reading plan to know and love God better.

Tara-Leigh speaks to a wide variety of audiences, and she regularly leads teaching trips to Israel because she loves to watch others be awed by the story of Scripture through firsthand experience.

Her favorite things include sparkling water and days that are 72 degrees with 55 percent humidity, and she thinks every meal tastes better when eaten outside. She lives in a concrete box in the skies of Dallas, Texas, where she has no pets, children, or anything that might die if she forgets to feed it.

For more information about Tara-Leigh and her ministry, you can visit her online:

Websites: taraleighcobble.com | thebiblerecap.com | mydgroup.org
Social media: @taraleighcobble | @thebiblerecap | @mydgroup

Also from Tara-Leigh Cobble

Have you ever closed your Bible and thought, *What did I just read?* In an easy-to-understand way, popular podcaster of *The Bible Recap* Tara-Leigh Cobble walks readers through a one-year chronological Bible reading plan, explaining each day's passage to help you both understand the entire narrative of the Scriptures and fortify your faith.

The Bible Recap

This attractive deluxe edition of *The Bible Recap* features an imitation leather cover, a ribbon marker, and a striking two-color interior. This makes the perfect gift for holidays, celebrations, or simply encouraging someone in their faith.

The Bible Recap, Deluxe Edition

Tie your study together with *The Bible Recap Journal*, which offers writing prompts and uniquely organized space perfect for recording and tracking each day through the whole Bible.

The Bible Recap Journal

BETHANYHOUSE

 Stay up to date on your favorite books and authors with our free e-newsletters. Sign up today at bethanyhouse.com.

 facebook.com/BHPnonfiction

 @bethany_house

 @bethany_house_nonfiction